TABLE OF CONTENTS

INTRODUCTION

The Office of Management and Budget (OMB) developed this report pursuant to section 732 of the *Consolidation Appropriations Act, 2012* (P.L. 112-74), as carried forward in the *Continuing Appropriations Act, 2014* (P.L. 113-46).[1] In accordance with the Act, this report provides a description of E-Government initiatives including the objectives, benefits, development status, risks, and cost effectiveness of E-Government initiatives and lines of business.

As required by the Act, this report includes the sources and distribution of FY 2014 funding by agency and by bureau. Prior year funding information is available in previous reports submitted to Congress, available online at: *www.WhiteHouse.gov/omb/e-gov/docs.* As explained in previous annual reports, estimated future contribution levels are unavailable as funding algorithms are determined annually by each initiative's governance board. Estimated annual operations and maintenance costs are also unavailable as initiative governance boards have not determined and voted upon the costs to operate in the out-years. Additionally, information regarding estimated dates of full operational capability and costs to complete an initiative's development is unavailable as E-Government initiatives and lines of business are evolutionary. While most initiatives have accomplished their initial goals and achieved operational capability, they have also expanded their goals over time, transitioning from individual projects to more robust programs. These programs are constantly evolving; there is no final date by which initiatives and lines of business are considered to have achieved full operational capability.

This report provides information regarding E-Government initiatives funded through agency contributions, and does not include all Federal government shared services. Agency contributions include commitments of funding and/or in-kind contributions, which represent the dollar-equivalent of a contribution of services, equipment, facilities, software, license fees, or Full-Time Equivalent (FTE) personnel support. Because the Act requires the report to include E-Government initiatives sponsored by OMB, initiatives funded through a "fee-for-service" model in which reimbursements represent transfers of funds by agencies to a service provider in exchange for a service rendered are not included in this report.[2]

This report is organized as follows:

Summary of E-Government Initiatives and Lines of Business
In accordance with section 732(b)(1) of the Act, this section provides a description of the objectives and primary benefits of E-Government initiatives and lines of business, and highlights the accomplishments and cost-effectiveness of the initiatives.

Appendix A: Examples of Agency-Specific Benefits
In accordance with section 732(b)(1) of the Act, this section provides highlights of agency-specific benefits of the initiatives.

Appendix B: Sources of FY 2014 E-Government Initiative and Lines of Business Funding by Department/Agency and Bureau
In accordance with section 732(b)(3) of the Act, this table shows FY 2014 department/agency contributions to E-Government initiatives and lines of business.

Appendix C: FY 2014 Funding by E-Government Initiative and Line of Business
In accordance with section 732(b)(3) of the Act, this table shows the distribution of FY 2014 department/agency contributions by initiative.

Appendix D: Development Status of E-Government Initiatives and Lines of Business
In accordance with section 732(b)(1) of the Act, this table shows the development status of E-Government initiatives and lines of business.

Appendix E: Risks Associated with E-Government Initiatives and Lines of Business
In accordance with section 732(b)(1) of the Act, this table shows the risks of E-Government initiatives and lines of business.

SUMMARY OF E-GOVERNMENT INITIATIVES AND LINES OF BUSINESS

In accordance with section 732(b)(1) of the Act, this section describes the objectives and primary benefits of E-Government initiatives, and highlights the accomplishments and cost-effectiveness of the initiatives. The information in this section is organized alphabetically by initiative name, and was developed in coordination with each initiative's managing partner and partner agencies.

Budget Formulation and Execution Line of Business (BFE LoB)

Managing Partner: U.S. Department of Education

Partner Agencies

Department of Agriculture	U.S. Agency for International Development
Department of Commerce	U.S. Army Corps of Engineers
Department of Defense	Broadcasting Board of Governors
Department of Energy	Environmental Protection Agency
Department of Health and Human Services	Equal Employment Opportunity Commission
Department of Homeland Security	General Services Administration
Department of Housing and	Millennium Challenge Corporation
Urban Development	National Aeronautics and Space
Department of the Interior	Administration
Department of Justice	National Science Foundation
Department of Labor	Office of National Drug Control Policy
Department of State	Office of Personnel Management
Department of Transportation	Securities and Exchange Commission
Department of the Treasury	Small Business Administration
Department of Veterans Affairs	

Objective

The focus of the BFE LoB is to continue to build a "budget office of the future," by promoting information sharing across government agency budget offices. The BFE LoB's goals include improvement and enhancements of:

- Efficiency and effectiveness of agency and central processes for formulating and executing the Federal Budget;

- Integrated and standardized exchange of budget formulation, execution, planning, performance measurement, and financial management information and activities across the government;

- Capabilities for analyzing budget formulation, execution, planning, performance, and financial information in support of decision-making; and,

- Capabilities for aligning programs, their outputs, and outcomes with budget levels and actual costs to institutionalize budget and performance integration.

Primary Benefits

The BFE LoB provides agencies with technological solutions, tools, and services for enhancing budgeting, analysis, document production, and data collection. The BFE LoB also provides tools for secure collaboration and online meetings, and human capital solutions. Through the BFE LoB, agencies can share best practices for budgeting activities, identify training and educational opportunities, and communicate core competencies and career path options for budget analysts. Finally, the BFE LoB provides governance solutions, providing year-round coordination via a program management office, furthering the idea of sharing and re-use, and setting standards for data and data exchange.

Accomplishments and Examples of Cost Effectiveness

- **MAX Federal Community and MAX Collect**

The BFE LoB continued the evolution of a governmentwide collaboration site, the MAX Federal Community, and a data collection tool, MAX Collect, to facilitate increased information gathering and sharing, collaboration, and knowledge management across the Federal government. The MAX Community allows users to share documents and data, and participate in real-time meetings through an open standards-based wiki platform using any Web browser. MAX Collect enables structured, web-based collection of data in multiple formats while providing analytics and publication capabilities.

The MAX Community is now the largest collaboration environment in the Federal government, serving over 90,000 registered users from over 150 agencies and components worldwide. Nearly 300 MAX Collect exercises have been created to support a range of data collection and publication activities, including the development of the President's Budget, agency responses to congressional Questions for the Record, and tracking Federal internet domain usage. For many agencies, the MAX Community is their only externally-facing collaboration vehicle. These tools enable agency budget officers to more effectively respond to data calls and questions. The MAX Community has yielded millions of dollars in cost-avoidance through the use of open-standards MAX applications, and cross-agency collaboration capabilities, avoiding duplicative investments.

- **Training Opportunities**

The BFE LoB sponsors various training classes, workshops and conferences for the Federal government budget community. The BFE LoB developed self-paced, online training modules pertaining to budget formulation, budget execution, and appropriations law. Federal employees can take the online courses at their own pace, download the course materials, print out the transcripts, or view the process maps upon which the courses are based. The BFE LoB invested roughly $120,000 to develop the online courses. By comparison, industry prices for the same quality of coursework are $800 to $1,000 per person, per class. By utilizing courses offered through the BFE LoB, agencies can potentially avoid $3.50-$4.50 million in training costs depending on the number of personnel per agency who would otherwise have to register for training with an outside entity.

In addition, the BFE LoB hosts monthly panel discussions with senior agency and OMB experts, quarterly mentoring, a semi-annual conference, and hands-on workshops to provide budget professionals numerous avenues for gaining a better understanding of Federal budgeting, and their role in the process. Approximately 4,700 Federal government employees have completed the online courses, over 1,500 have attended the monthly and quarterly sessions, and another 1,500 employees from over 30 agencies have attended the semi-annual conferences.

Disaster Assistance Improvement Program (DAIP)

Managing Partner: U.S. Department of Homeland Security
Partner Agencies

Department of Agriculture	Department of Labor
Department of Commerce	Department of State
Department of Education	Department of the Treasury
Department of Health and Human Services	Department of Veterans Affairs
Department of Housing and Urban Development	Office of Personnel Management
Department of the Interior	Small Business Administration
Department of Justice	Social Security Administration

Objective

The objective of the DAIP is to simplify the process of identifying and applying for disaster assistance as required by President George W. Bush's Executive Order of August 29, 2006, *Improving Assistance for Disaster Victims.*[3] The DAIP created *www.DisasterAssistance.gov*, a website that consolidates disaster assistance information and application interfaces from multiple Federal forms of assistance (FOAs) in one place. This website enabled individuals in need of assistance following a presidentially declared disaster to register for assistance online.

Primary Benefits

Seventeen Federal agencies currently contribute to the portal, which offers application information for approximately 71 FOAs, as well as news, information and resources to help individuals, families and businesses prepare for, respond to, and recover from disasters. DAIP enhances data sharing among partner agencies, which simplifies the application process for survivors. From October 1, 2012, through August 31, 2013, *www.DisasterAssistance.gov* processed 4,004,063 page views of partner agency disaster assistance information (an increase from the 1,574,401 page views processed in FY 2012), and 1,303,670 data sharing transactions between Federal Emergency Management Agency (FEMA) and interfacing partner agencies (an increase from the 285,758 transactions processed in FY 2012).

Additional benefits of *www.DisasterAssistance.gov* include:

- Reduced number of forms users complete when applying for assistance;

- Shortens application time by providing assistance through an online questionnaire, which identifies opportunities to apply for assistance from multiple federal agencies; and,

- Allows users to upload supporting documents related to their application (versus mailing paper records), monitor the status of their application online, and receive status updates via SMS text messaging.

DAIP also reduces development costs incurred by partner agencies. Partner agencies have benefited from the cost-savings related to the development of the enterprise architecture which supports _www. DisasterAssistance.gov_. The portal decreases labor hours, provides automated tracking, reduces fraud, waste and abuse, and improves information sharing. DAIP also developed a cross-agency service oriented architecture platform, and is developing a federated application that allows partner agencies to interface with the program without costly modifications to their own network architecture. The near 100% uptime infrastructure provides partner agencies with a high level of service while avoiding costs of operating independently.

DAIP actively conducts outreach about _www.DisasterAssistance.gov_ services to stakeholders and communities prior to and immediately following disasters and also works internally with partner agencies' public affairs groups to share information and updates about the site. Continued investment in DAIP will enable future improvements to _www.DisasterAssistance.gov_, and enhance the services and information available on the site.

Accomplishments and Examples of Cost Effectiveness

- **Improved Mobile Device Capabilities**

In FY 2013, _www.DisasterAssistance.gov_ continued to experience high site usage and volume. Although FY 2013 was a relatively quiet hurricane season, flooding and drought emergencies across the country led to an increase in site usage in the third and early fourth quarter of the fiscal year. The percentage of users accessing _www.DisasterAssistance.gov_ via a mobile device also continued to increase in FY 2013. Prior to Hurricanes Sandy and Isaac in FY 2012, only 4% of applicant inquiries came from mobile devices. Following those hurricanes, the percentage increased to 25%. In FY 2013, 32% of applicant inquiries came from mobile devices. DAIP estimates the trend will continue, and has made mobile improvements a priority for the program moving forward. The program has optimized the website for mobile viewing through the universal page rendering site optimization project, and added SMS text messaging capabilities for application status changes. These changes have increased the distribution of disaster assistance information, and provided rapid access to applications and FOA's through _www. DisasterAssistance.gov_.

- **Improving the User Experience**

DAIP took a governmentwide approach to providing cross-agency disaster assistance while improving the user experience. DAIP made improvements to the portal questionnaire, tailoring recommendations based on how users answered questions. The tool allows users to search FOA's by category or agency. Users can sort, tag and find more information on specific FOA's, and then print or email their results. Upon completing the questionnaire, a survivor can register for assistance online and return to DisasterAssistance.gov later to check the status of their registration. From October 1, 2011, through August 31, 2013, survivors used _www.DisasterAssistance.gov_ to complete 1,049,600 unique questionnaires, 42% of which turned into applications for assistance.

Prior to the development of _www.DisasterAssistance.gov_, disaster survivors had to use separate application procedures for each agency from which they were requesting assistance. Development of the site reduces the amount of time required to apply for, and check the status of, federal assistance, while at the same time reducing processing time and costs to the federal government. Between January and August 2013, survivors took an average of 18 minutes to complete the online registration process, 19 minutes when using a mobile device, and 21 minutes when registering through the FEMA call center. DAIP uses survivor feedback collected from phone and online surveys, usability studies, analytics data, and partner agency guidance to make improvements to _www.DisasterAssistance.gov_, and further simplify the disaster assistance process for survivors.

In addition, in FY 2013 DAIP added three new pages to _www.DisasterAssistance.gov_ highlighting the specific needs of children and families, older Americans, and individuals with disabilities or access and functional needs, in an effort to be better prepared before, during and after a disaster. The new pages include valuable content, and links to resources from various federal partners, state emergency management groups and nonprofit organizations.

Disaster Management (DM) Program

> Managing Partner: U.S. Department of Homeland Security
> (No Partner Agencies)

Objective

The role of the DM program is to offer innovative, effective, and efficient solutions to deliver information and services related to disasters for citizens and members of the emergency management community at the Federal, state, local, tribal, and territorial levels. The program focuses on achieving greater cost efficiency, improving access to key disaster preparedness and assistance information, and instituting an agency-wide, web-centric culture for information sharing and collaboration. The DM program ensures information relevant to disaster survivors, the general public, and the emergency management community is organized and presented in a manner that engages and improves the overall user experience.

Primary Benefits

The DM program identifies opportunities for the Federal government to procure and manage devices, applications, and data in smart, secure, and affordable ways, and technology innovations which improve the quality of services and data utilized by the public. The DM program adopted a new enterprise-wide digital media and asset management solution that incorporates standards and processes for creating, storing, and sharing assets. This solution allows for the adoption of a new customer relation and correspondence management system, which provides a platform for managing correspondence and information-sharing with the public. It also allows for continued enhancements to the FEMA Mobile App, including Disaster Reporter, which enables the public to access high-quality, digital government information and services anytime, on any device. These initiatives contribute to cost reductions, centralization, improved workflow, and an information-centric approach which allows for more efficient and effective management of open data and content, as well as shared platforms which may be leveraged at the enterprise level.

Accomplishments and Examples of Cost Effectiveness

- **Digital Imagery and Media On-Demand (DIAMOND) Application**

The DIAMOND application is a cloud-based system for the storage, management, and organization of digital media files. This application was launched in July 2013 as a pilot system to support FEMA's digital media requirements. The initiative is part of DHS's effort to move data to the cloud in order to reduce costs. Over 6,000 document container records and 26,187 total assets were migrated to DIAMOND in August 2013, and the multimedia migration launched in September 2013. More than 100 people have been trained to use DIAMOND documents and reference guides, and simulations have been developed to aid users.

- **Mobile Device Capabilities and Website Upgrades**

The FEMA Mobile App provides functionality and information-sharing for the public and all levels of government across multiple devices and platforms. Specifically, the Disaster Reporter functionality allows for crowdsourcing and sharing disaster-related information for events occurring within the U.S. This functionality is compatible with Android, iOS, and BlackBerry devices. In addition, the DM program has made improvements to various websites, including adding seven languages to _www.Ready. gov_, providing citizens with multilingual content, and launching the new _www.Ready.gov/kids_ website. The DM program has also implemented social media monitoring and analysis tools, which provide a method for DHS and FEMA to analyze, measure, display, and create reports based on information collected through multiple streams of social media.

Federal Asset Sales (FAS)

Managing Partner: General Services Administration   (No Partner Agencies)

Objective

FAS manages a one-stop online marketplace known as GovSales for Federal agencies to sell underutilized, non-utilized, replacement and forfeited assets. GovSales also serves as a single online marketplace for the public to search for personal property and real property assets for sale across the Federal government. The public is able to search GovSales for property regardless of whether the item is available for sale online, or offline via live auction or other method of sale.

Primary Benefits

Electronic Federal Asset Sales (eFAS) has improved the way the Federal government disposes of unneeded assets. FAS previously established seven sales centers authorizing agencies to sell real and/or personal property on behalf of the Federal government. GSA, the Department of Agriculture, the Department of Defense, the Department of the Interior Office of Aviation Management, the Department of Justice U.S. Marshals Service, and the Department of the Treasury Internal Revenue Service and Asset Forfeiture Division all serve as authorized sales centers that other Federal agencies use to dispose of surplus, forfeited, and exchange/sale personal property. It provides Federal agencies with a standardized mechanism to sell government-owned property, and enables agencies to reach a broader customer base and obtain greater exposure for their assets during disposal. Automating the disposal process reduces cycle time, saving storage and transportation expenses. In addition, GovSales provides citizens with a consolidated inventory of real and personal property from multiple sales centers to make it easier to search for and buy assets.

Accomplishments and Examples of Cost Effectiveness

- **Broadening the Customer Base**

FAS enables agencies and bureaus with limited resources to leverage economies of scale to reach a broader customer base, and improve the promotion of government assets for sale. The volume of property sold through GovSales is significant. For FY 2011, 474,226 items were sold, with gross sales of $571,091,693. In FY 2012, 514,408 items were sold, with gross sales of $580,406,601. FY 2013 sales will not be reported until December 31, 2013, and are unavailable for this report.

As part of a continuous effort to improve customer outreach, FAS restructures their marketing strategies on an annual basis. In FY 2013, FAS placed ads in the USA Today Magazine and other media outlets, placed ads on billboards, and enhanced their social media outreach efforts. In addition, FAS conducts public outreach via marketing booths at state fairs, trade shows, and conferences nationwide. Such events allow FAS to showcase the GovSales web portal, and target specific audiences that may benefit from FAS. In FY 2012, FAS was able to reach over 2 million citizens and bring awareness to GovSales. Although restrictions on travel reduced FAS's presence at these events in FY 2013, FAS continued public outreach at state fairs, and promoted awareness of GovSales to the general public. Increases in web portal traffic immediately following the outreach events are evident, indicating these events are driving more members of the public to the web portal. Increased web traffic could potentially lead to an increase in sales, although sales are not directly associated with the amount of website views.

Federal Health Architecture Line of Business (FHA LoB)

Managing Partner: U.S. Department of Health and Human Services

Partner Agencies

Department of Defense   Social Security Administration

Department of Veterans Affairs

Objective

The FHA LoB is a partnership among federal agencies and OMB, and is managed by the Office of the National Coordinator for Health IT (ONC). The U.S. Department of Health & Human Services (HHS) collaborates with partner agencies to advance health information interoperability between Federal agencies, and tribal, state, local and private sectors. The FHA LoB serves the needs of more than twenty Federal agencies in domains as diverse as military and veterans' healthcare, public health monitoring, long-term care and disability services, research, tribal health services and many other critical Federal priorities.

Primary Benefits

Through the FHA LoB, Federal agencies are able to rapidly and efficiently coordinate government-wide solutions for an interoperable and secure health information exchange that addresses agency priorities, while protecting citizen privacy. FHA facilitates coordination between Federal agencies to support alignment of health IT investments, including the CONNECT Gateway project, the Federal Health Interoperability Modeling (FHIM) initiative, Federal Health Information Planning and Reporting (FHIPR) and other projects. These initiatives have led to the development of an integrated set of standards that support health information interoperability, guidance to enable agencies to plan health IT investments, and information to help agencies identify and select health IT solutions that align to national health IT interoperability guidelines and standards.

Accomplishments and Examples of Cost Effectiveness

- **Support of the Social Security Administration (SSA) Disability Program**

The SSA disability program processes approximately three million disability applications each year. To process these applications, SSA makes about 15 million patient-authorized requests for medical information from health care providers. SSA is utilizing the Medical Evidence Gathering and Analysis through Health IT (MEGAHIT) project to migrate the healthcare documentation process from paper-based to electronic format. This project has improved the speed and quality of the disability determination process by automating both the authorized requests and receipt of data. SSA has demonstrated operational improvements, including a 14% (or 13 day) reduction in initial case processing time for health IT disability cases. Reducing the amount of time to receive medical evidence from weeks to minutes significantly improves the time it takes for claimants to receive disability benefits.

SSA has also partnered with healthcare organizations to enable the electronic exchange of health information through the eHealth Exchange, which improves the speed and effectiveness of the disability decision-making process. The exchange allows medical providers to receive a standardized electronic request for medical records, and automatically respond to SSA with structured medical information. In FY 2013, SSA expanded the exchange to 20 active health IT partners who provided access to numerous medical sources.

- **Virtual Lifetime Electronic Record (VLER)**

The VLER initiative remains a top priority for the Department of Defense (DOD), and the Department of Veterans Affairs (VA). When fully developed, VLER will support the sharing of comprehensive health, benefit and personal information through a secure query, which complies with various national standards including those of the eHealth Exchange, Standards and Interoperability Framework, and the Health Information Technology Standards and Panel.

DOD and VA have continued to leverage the improvements FHA has made in the CONNECT Gateway software to expand partnerships with private sector health care providers and Health Information Exchange (HIE) organizations. DOD and VA have established multiple VLER Health pilot locations where their beneficiaries' health information can be shared among the two departments and private sector partners. Access to this information can potentially reduce duplication of tests and improve treatment and overall quality of care. DOD and VA plan to expand the capability to additional locations in FY 2014. As part of this effort, these departments plan also to update the CONNECT software in FY 2014.

A second VLER Health initiative is the Direct Secure Messaging project. Direct Secure Messaging is a point-to-point "push" of clinical information using secure email over a trusted network. DOD implemented a Direct Secure Messaging pilot at the 75th Medical Group at Hill Air Force Base in Ogden, Utah. The pilot tested the security, privacy, and trust of the direct secure email used to provide clear and legible reports of mammogram results for TRICARE patients from McKay Dee Hospital to the 75th Medical Group. The VA plans to implement a similar pilot in early 2014.

DOD also developed and began testing a Direct as a Service Application Programming Interface as a transport mechanism to facilitate patient mediated exchange. Through this capability, service members and veterans will be able to use the Blue Button feature of *TRICARE Online* or *MyHealtheVet* to securely send a continuity of care document from their personal health record to a third party electronic health record of their choice using Direct Secure Messaging. To support this activity, FHA sponsored a series of ongoing discussions through a Directed Exchange Work Group, bringing Federal partners together to develop a Federal Public Key Infrastructure security certificate policy, which will be used by the Direct Secure Messaging project to expand HIE activity with private sector health care and Health Information Service Provider organizations.

Financial Management Line of Business (FM LoB)

Managing Partner: U.S. Department of the Treasury
Partner Agencies

Department of Agriculture	Department of Transportation
Department of Commerce	Department of Veterans Affairs
Department of Defense	U.S. Agency for International Development
Department of Education	Environmental Protection Agency
Department of Energy	General Services Administration
Department of Health and Human Services	National Aeronautics and Space Administration
Department of Homeland Security	Nuclear Regulatory Commission
Department of Housing and Urban Development	National Science Foundation
Department of the Interior	Office of Personnel Management
Department of Justice	Small Business Administration
Department of Labor	Social Security Administration
Department of State	

Objective

The objective of the FM LoB is to define, analyze, and implement options to improve financial management systems solutions for the financial management community using a "shared first" approach, and to further Financial Centers of Excellence. The FM LoB leverages lessons learned to inform shared service planning, and decision making for other key functions, such as financial assistance and acquisitions.

FM LoB serves to standardize, optimize, and consolidate Federal financial management systems to improve the cost, quality, and performance of financial management systems by leveraging shared services solutions and by implementing other governmentwide reforms that foster efficiencies in Federal financial operations and improved public reporting of Federal financial data.

Primary Benefits

The FM LoB supports governmentwide efforts to improve the reliability and accessibility of public and internal financial data through standardization of data elements and development of resources to support a well-qualified workforce.

Furthermore, the FM LoB provides funding and resources to improve governmentwide financial management initiatives for real property, federal spending transparency, and identification of opportunities to streamline financial management processes within various Centers of Excellence (i.e. grants, loans, fixed assets, etc.). The FM LoB supports agency implementation of Federal financial management systems and other reforms that:

- Facilitate stronger internal controls to ensure integrity in accounting and other stewardship activities;

- Reduce costs by enabling agencies to implement and operate financial management systems through shared service provider solutions;

- Standardize systems, business processes, and data elements; and,

- Close performance gaps in Federal financial management.

The FM LoB saves taxpayer dollars, improves public reporting of Federal financial data, reduces administrative burdens, reduces the risk of waste, fraud, and abuse, and significantly improves financial management services across the government.

Accomplishments and Examples of Cost Effectiveness

- **Transferring Authority to the Office of Financial Innovation and Transformation**

The Department of the Treasury assumed responsibility of the FM LoB from GSA in FY 2013. Transferring the initiative to Treasury enables the Office of Financial Innovation and Transformation (FIT) to lead efforts to transform Federal financial management by reducing duplicative work at multiple agencies, devising new automated solutions, and assisting OMB in developing a long-term financial management systems strategy.

FIT is working with agency Chief Financial Officers to ensure that each agency is positioned to adopt a shared service approach. FIT will work with the agencies to evaluate any new systems modernization plans and requirements, and maintain core governmentwide financial standards while limiting expansion and impact on financial system requirements. FIT also works to identify and facilitate the implementation of governmentwide operational capabilities (e.g., invoice processing and centralized receivables management) that help reduce costs and increase transparency. The ongoing efforts to standardize, optimize, and consolidate agency financial systems will decrease redundancy and drive cost-savings through development, modernization, and enhancement.

- **Federal Audit Clearinghouse**

The FM LoB supported the U.S. Census Bureau's Single Audit work for the Federal Audit Clearinghouse (FAC). The FAC is operated by the Census Bureau on behalf of OMB. Its primary purposes are to distribute single audit reporting packages to Federal agencies, support OMB oversight and assessment of Federal award audit requirements, maintain a public database of completed audits, and help to minimize the reporting burden associated with complying with *OMB Circular A-133, "Audits of States, Local Governments, and Non-Profit Organizations."* Through the FM LoB, Federal agency personnel received training on the FAC, and were able to provide customer support to Federal agencies and auditors.

Support of the FAC also improved the internet data entry system for the collection of single audit forms, and enabled a redesign of the FAC audit forms processing system. Improving these systems allowed the Federal government to gain efficiencies in submissions and reporting, and reduced the amount of time and resources spent on submissions.

Geospatial Line of Business (Geo LoB)

Managing Partner: U.S. Department of the Interior

Partner Agencies

Department of Agriculture	Department of Veterans Affairs
Department of Commerce	U.S. Agency for International Development
Department of Defense	U.S. Army Corps of Engineers
Department of Education	Environmental Protection Agency
Department of Energy	General Services Administration
Department of Health and Human Services	National Aeronautics and Space Administration
Department of Homeland Security	National Archives and Records Administration
Department of Housing and Urban Development	National Science Foundation
Department of Justice	Small Business Administration
Department of State	Social Security Administration
Department of Transportation	
Department of the Treasury	

Objective

The objective of the Geo LoB is to provide cross-agency coordination, and identify opportunities for optimizing and consolidating Federal geospatial-related investments. The Geo LoB seeks to improve sharing of geospatial information, and reduce costs by avoiding the creation of duplicative geospatial information. The Geo Lob also enables partner agencies to collaborate and apply geospatial information, and provides services to support national defense priorities.

Primary Benefits

Sharing data, services, and applications through the Geo LoB lowers costs for data, hardware and software, increases the volume of data shared with the public. The Geo LoB helps the geospatial community continue to serve as leaders in the implementation of publishing services for open government data.

Accomplishments and Examples of Cost Effectiveness

- **Advancement of the Geospatial Platform**

The volume of geospatial information made available to Geo LoB partner agencies and the general public has increased through the expanded use of the *Geospatial Platform*. The Geospatial Platform offers access to trusted geospatial data, services, and applications managed in the Federal Geospatial Portfolio to support Federal, state, local, and tribal governments in meeting their mission objectives, and provide efficiencies and cost savings through shared infrastructure and enterprise solutions.

The Geo LoB successfully transitioned to the Geospatial Platform Version 2 which allowed the advancement of a collaborative effort to support geospatial activities across Federal agencies, and helps to improve the efficiency of government by making geospatial data more accessible, reliable, and less expensive to acquire through enhanced data-sharing and more effective management of resources.

The Geospatial Platform was integrated with _www.Data.gov_, a resource which increases public access to high value, machine readable datasets generated by the Executive Branch of the Federal Government. The Geospatial Platform has also focused on the advancement of "Communities," and the integration of the new Geospatial Platform Marketplace. The Geospatial Platform Marketplace is a new feature which allows agencies to post information regarding their planned geospatial data acquisitions for their partners to be able to view in an effort to facilitate collaboration and shared acquisition for data that are of interest among multiple agencies. "Communities" are sections of the website designed specifically for collaboration within communities of interest where users can highlight and share their maps, data and tools. For example, the National Blueway System Community provides a portal for data, information, and resources to support people engaged in efforts to make rivers and watersheds healthy and resilient. Additionally, the Geo LoB has been instrumental in advancing the development of the new Strategic Plan for the National Spatial Data Infrastructure, a major initiative that will bring the Department of the Interior (DOI) and all Geo LoB partner agencies considerable benefits for years to come.

Human Resources Line of Business (HR LoB)

Managing Partner: Office of Personnel Management
Partner Agencies

Department of Agriculture	Department of State
Department of Commerce	Department of Transportation
Department of Defense	Department of the Treasury
Department of Education	Department of Veterans Affairs
Department of Energy	U.S. Agency for International Development
Department of Health and Human Services	Central Intelligence Agency
Department of Homeland Security	Environmental Protection Agency
Department of Housing and Urban Development	General Services Administration
Department of the Interior	National Aeronautics and Space Administration
Department of Justice	National Science Foundation
Department of Labor	

Objective

The objective of the HR LoB is to lead the governmentwide transformation of HR information technology by focusing on modernization, integration, and performance assessment. The HR LoB vision is to create governmentwide, modern, cost-effective, standardized, and interoperable HR solutions to provide common core functionality in support of the strategic management of HR through the establishment of a shared services delivery model for the Federal government.

Primary Benefits

The HR LoB initiative enables the consolidation, standardization, and modernization of human resources information technology (HRIT). As the HR LoB continues to move forward with agency migrations to the approved shared service centers (SSCs), the Federal government will continue to realize the benefits of improved management, operational efficiency, and improved customer service.

Accomplishments and Examples of Cost Effectiveness

- **Provider Assessment**

The HR LoB launched the Provider Assessment, a business practice-based assessment that appraises HR LoB service providers on their ability to deliver services to their customers. The Provider Assessment determines how well Federal HR SSCs and payroll providers operate and provide services to their customers. The Provider Assessment also includes a customer satisfaction component, measuring the extent to which Federal customers are satisfied with HR and payroll services and business practices.

The Provider Assessment yields the following important outcomes:

- Ensures providers are delivering appropriate levels of customer service and customers are satisfied with their provider's service delivery;

- Verifies that providers are compliant with Federal laws, regulations, policies, and accepted practices;

- Increases visibility into provider operating practices, procedures, and supporting technology in order to build a foundation of trust and openness among providers and customers, resulting in more efficient, effective HR operations; and,

- Influences providers to move toward modern, cost-effective, standardized, and interoperable HR solutions.

The Provider Assessment ensures that agencies receive high-quality services and systems for a fraction of the cost as they migrate to SSCs. Additionally, the transparency resulting from the assessment will lead to significantly more savings as agencies look to further reduce duplication by migrating non-core HR systems to SSCs. This reduction will improve agency HR business processing, reducing the amount of labor hours needed for administrative processing activities, and enabling HR specialists to focus on mission-oriented HR activities.

- **Migration to Shared Service Centers**

The HR LoB has established six public, and four private sector shared service centers (SSCs) which offer governmentwide HR technology solutions, and provide valuable strategic and consultative support for agency missions. The SSCs leverage economies of scale, reduce costs, and increase the quality and consistency of HR services provided to agencies.

Agency migration to an approved SSC reduces the amount of resources spent on implementing or upgrading internal HR IT systems. The HR LoB supports agencies in their selection of and migration to SSCs, consistent with the business model determined by the agency. The HR LoB also provides oversight of the SSCs through governance and performance assessments, including monthly assessments, and monitoring the cost, schedule and performance of on-going migrations.

In FY 2013, the Department of Commerce, Department of Labor, Department of Veterans Affairs, and the Environmental Protection Agency all began migrating to an SSC during FY 2013. The HR LoB also approved HHS to begin migration to an SSC. By doing so, agencies are able to transition their internal HR efforts from administrative processes, to strategic planning, operational efficiencies, reducing costs, supporting agency leadership, improving customer service, and providing counseling for managers and employees.

Information Systems Security Line of Business (ISS LoB)

Managing Partner: U.S. Department of Homeland Security
(No Partner Agencies)

Objective

The ISS LoB is a governmentwide initiative that provides leadership and direction for improving effectiveness and consistency of information systems security across the Federal government. Its charter is to analyze current government sector conditions, determine immediate and root causes of security vulnerabilities, and provide leadership for mitigating those causes. The ISS LoB seeks to develop common solutions in the form of products and/or managed services that can be utilized governmentwide to address information systems security mandates, policy, and guidance from the National Institute of Standards and Technology (NIST).

Primary Benefits

The tools and services offered through the ISS LoB-sponsored acquisitions are priced lower than those available through other vehicles. The security tools and services provided by the ISS LoB are prioritized by agency stakeholders. For each ISS LoB-sponsored acquisition, the ISS LoB program management officer engages stakeholders to develop requirements, which are then submitted to acquisition partners, such as GSA, for the development of a formal Request for Quotation (RFQ). These acquisition partners make evaluations, award contracts, and make modifications to the contracts or requirements as needed.

The ISS LoB also offers tools and services to agencies through SSCs. The SSCs are Federal agencies with expertise in particular security offerings that are available to peer agencies at rates lower than those of comparable private sector services. The ISS LoB currently oversees six SSCs which provide risk management services, and four SSCs which offer security awareness training services to the Federal community. These SSCs submit bi-annual metrics to the ISS LoB, and are assessed on an annual basis to ensure that they continue to meet ISS LoB standards of excellence.

Accomplishments and Examples of Cost Effectiveness

- **Continuous Monitoring as a Service (CMaaS)**

The CMaaS family of acquisitions provides information security tools and services that meet the needs and priorities of agency stakeholders. CMaaS enhances security while providing cost-avoidance in the IT security arena. The CMaaS Blanket Purchase Agreement (BPA), awarded in the fourth quarter of FY 2013, is a toolset which encompasses greater capabilities than the original Situational Awareness and Incident Response (SAIR) BPA. The CMaaS BPA covers the following 15 continuous monitoring capabilities:

1. Hardware inventory management

2. Software inventory management

3. Configuration setting management

4. Vulnerability management

5. Network/physical access control management

6. Trust-in-people granted access (Access Control Management)

7. Security-related behavior management

8. Quality management

9. Credentials and authentication management

10. Privilege management

11. Prepare for incidents and contingencies

12. Respond to incidents and contingencies

13. Requirements, policy, and planning

14. Operational security

15. Generic audit/monitoring

The CMaaS BPA saves time and resources by eliminating the need for agencies to develop requirements, formulate a statement of work, solicit RFQ responses, and conduct full-scale evaluations for these offerings. In FY 2013, agencies saved an average of 88% in acquisition costs when by utilizing the CMaaS BPA. For example, one agency purchased a license for a systems lifecycle solution. The agency purchased 370,000 licenses which have an MSRP of $19.80. Using the BPA pricing, however, the cost per license was $2.39, which allowed the agency to achieve nearly $6.50 million in cost-savings.

- **SSC Risk Management and Security Awareness Training Services**
The ISS LoB offers standardized risk management and security awareness training to Federal civilian agencies through their SSCs. Using SSC services requires inter-agency agreements between SSCs and customer agencies, which are more streamlined than conducting a private sector acquisition of similar tools and services. Agencies save time and resources by utilizing risk management solutions and security awareness training through SSCs. Without SSC offerings, agencies would have to use internal resources, or procure private-sector offerings for these services. The commercial vendor rate for authorization and accreditation services is $127.47 per hour, and $26.00 per trainee for security awareness training, compared to the free services offered to Federal agencies by the ISS LoB. Using these rates as a baseline measurement, in FY 2013 the risk management and training services provided by the ISS LoB SSCs resulted in $84.10 million in cost-avoidance across the Federal government. Agencies have also saved hundreds of labor hours in development and implementation resources by leveraging security awareness training offerings to complete FISMA-required annual security training.

Additionally, by utilizing SSCs departments and agencies are able to procure services within weeks as opposed to months. In FY 2013, 58 agencies and their sub-components improved their security posture by using SSC risk management services to evaluate the technical and non-technical security controls of their information systems. SSC risk management services were used to determine if systems met specified security requirements, and thereby receive approval to operate at an acceptable level of risk, based on the implementation of an approved set of technical, managerial, and procedural security controls.

Internal Revenue Service (IRS) Free File

> Managing Partner: U.S. Department of the Treasury
> (No Partner Agencies)

Objective

The IRS Free File program allows eligible taxpayers to prepare and electronically file their Federal tax returns over the internet using commercial software for free. This free filing service is available at *www.IRS.gov*, and is made possible through a partnership between the government and the Free File Alliance, a consortium of tax preparation software manufacturers. Free File Alliance members must meet the privacy and security standards required by the IRS.

Primary Benefits

Since the inception of the Free File program in 2003, nearly 40 million returns have been successfully e-filed. For the 2013 filing season, Free File has delivered over 2.9 million returns. Assuming an average cost of $30 for a basic, do-it-yourself Federal tax return software product, it is estimated that $1.20 billion worth of free services have been provided by the Free File Alliance. In addition, the IRS Free File initiative has led to the growth of a free tax preparation marketplace, one that did not exist prior to the advent of Free File.

The Free File program also achieves IRS cost-savings, and provides financial savings to taxpayers. According to the Advancing e-file study, a paper return costs $2.52 more to process than one filed electronically. Using this unit cost savings, since its inception in 2003, IRS Free File has generated cost-savings to the government of approximately $101.0 million. This year's government savings are approximately $7.0 million.

The Free File program continues to be improved. Free File participants migrated from the Electronic Management System to Modernized e-file (MeF) during the 2013 filing season. Migration to MeF provides several key benefits for taxpayers, including faster acknowledgements of received returns, and improved error explanations.

Accomplishments and Examples of Cost Effectiveness

- **Free File Fillable Forms**
The Free File Fillable Forms utility is available to individual taxpayers at no charge, and without limitations by income. This utility provides electronic forms that resemble IRS paper forms. Taxpayers use the forms to prepare and electronically file their Federal tax returns through the Free File program. Free File provides a free option for taxpayers most comfortable with preparing a paper tax

return, and for taxpayers who do not meet software eligibility requirements. The program performs basic math calculations and transfers data between tax schedules and the Form 1040.

The utility offers nearly all of the individual 1040 tax forms and schedules. Since its introduction in 2009, 1.90 million returns have been e-filed using this utility. The volume of accepted returns associated with this utility has grown from 273,000 in 2009, to 475,000 in 2012. To date, 462,000 returns have been filed electronically using this utility for the 2013 filing season.

Recreation One-Stop

Managing Partner: U.S. Department of Agriculture

Partner Agencies

Department of the Interior | U.S. Army Corps of Engineers

Objective

The goal of the Recreation One-Stop initiative is to provide a comprehensive, customer-friendly recreation web portal, _www.Recreation.gov_, with information for planning visits to Federal recreation sites and making campground or tour reservations. Recreation One-Stop also seeks to provide consistent information about Federal recreation areas via different channels (databases, websites, and publications), and standardize data and interfacing recreation-related computer systems.

Primary Benefits

The Recreation.gov portal enables the public to make advance reservations for thousands of facilities such as day use areas, cabins, wilderness permits, tours, etc., via the internet, or by calling a toll free number. The _www.Recreation.gov_ website also provides electronic methods of payment, while ensuring payment card industry standards are met for secure credit card transactions, and that IT certification and accreditation requirements are met. This reduces cash handling for agency field sites which improves monetary accountability, safety and cost effectiveness. Advance reservations also reduce the burden on field site personnel to set up, and administer reservation services at individual sites and parks. Additionally, _www.Recreation.gov_ provides visitors and partners with one-stop access to maps, recreation activities and other useful federal lands information. The USDA administers the contract with Recreation.gov on behalf of seven Federal land management agencies, including the National Park Service, U.S. Army Corps of Engineers, U.S. Forest Service, U.S. Fish and Wildlife, the Bureau of Land Management, the Bureau of Reclamation and the National Archives.

Accomplishments and Examples of Cost Effectiveness

- **Improvements to Recreation.gov Web Portal**

In FY 2013, the content on the web portal was expanded to include additional trip planning tools such as destination itineraries, targeted lists of activities throughout the country and outdoor recreation related articles. Agencies are continuously expanding the information available of Recreation.gov to enhance recreation information and reservation opportunities. For example, in 2013, the National Park Service added new facilities and reservation opportunities on Recreation.gov at Fire Island National Seashore, Haleakala National Park, Prince William Forest Park, Colorado National Monument and Dinosaur National Monument. The U.S. Forest Service also added interpretive tour tickets to the new Chimney Rock National Monument.

In addition, the "Share the Experience" interagency photo contest, co-sponsored by Active Network and the National Park Foundation, concluded in FY 2013. The contest, which provides the annual image for the America the Beautiful Interagency Pass Program, received three times the number of photo entries than the previous contest period. Increased participation has provided extensive marketing to outdoor enthusiasts and a tremendous catalogue of images that can be used to market public lands.

- **Recreation Information Database (RIDB)**

The RIDB provides a single point of access to information about recreational opportunities nationwide. The RIDB integrates multiple sources of data into a robust, searchable database that can be used by Federal agencies, state tourism offices, and the public free of charge. The public can look for recreational opportunities in a specific geographic area and obtain all necessary information without having to visit multiple web sites. This simplifies trip planning and allows the public to see locations they might not have otherwise considered. As a result, the agencies achieve higher visibility of their campgrounds and sites, which leads to increased usage and occupancy. The U.S. Forest Service awarded the RIDB contract to a different vendor at a significantly reduced cost, saving nearly $500,000 over the five-year contract term. During the first period of performance, the data sharing capabilities of the RIDB have greatly improved. The management of high demand sites has also improved, along with the marketing and utilization of lesser known sites.

SAFECOM

Managing Partner: U.S. Department of Homeland Security
(No Partner Agencies)

Objective

SAFECOM is an intergovernmental Federal advisory committee within DHS, established in 2001 in response to the lack of emergency response interoperability. Although several government programs had made strides in addressing the issues pertaining to emergency response interoperability, much of the work was disconnected, fragmented, and often conflicting. SAFECOM facilitates the input of local and state emergency response practitioners.

The Office of Emergency Communications (OEC), a division within the National Protection and Programs Directorate, develops policy, guidance, and future efforts by drawing on SAFECOM member expertise and recommendations. The Office for Interoperability and Compatibility (OIC), an office within the Science and Technology Directorate, supports SAFECOM-related research, development, testing, and evaluation, as well as the acceleration of standards. These efforts achieve a shared vision, advance coordination, and defined long-term goals within the emergency communications community.

Primary Benefits

Through semi-annual meetings and regular working groups, SAFECOM has been responsible for developing numerous planning, guidance, and policy documents. SAFECOM members have contributed to the development of guidance documents such as the annual SAFECOM Guidance on Emergency Communications Grants, Statewide Communication Interoperability Plan (SCIP) Methodology, and the Public Safety Communications Evolution Brochure. Since its inception SAFECOM has taken a stakeholder-driven approach to achieving its mission of advancing interoperable communications across all levels of government—Federal, state, local, and tribal. In collaboration with over 60,000 distinct emergency response agencies across the country, SAFECOM provides a representative, formalized, and regular process to obtain input and feedback on its activities.

SAFECOM created the Emergency Response Council (ERC) and Executive Committee (EC) to ensure emergency communications stakeholders have a voice in the development of nationwide planning efforts and an opportunity to present input on user needs and resources. SAFECOM convenes the ERC and EC on a regular basis through webinars, teleconference and in-person meetings in order to provide stakeholder input on key initiatives and activities. In addition, SAFECOM developed strategic priorities and established corresponding working groups, including: Broadband Outreach; Next Generation 911; Funding and Sustainment; Land Mobile Radio (LMR) and Planning; and SAFECOM Outreach and Education.

The SAFECOM program has also resulted in several key emergency communications initiatives including development of the National Emergency Communications Plan (NECP), the Nation's first strategic plan to enhance emergency communications, and the SAFECOM Interoperability Continuum, a tool developed by emergency responders that identifies critical elements that must be addressed to achieve optimal interoperable conditions to respond to an event.

Accomplishments and Examples of Cost Effectiveness

- **Public Safety Communications Evolution**

By conducting strategic planning at the national level and leveraging statewide communication interoperability plans, duplication of costs and efforts can be kept to a minimum for all stakeholders. Also, through effective planning, coordination, and guidance stakeholders are also better prepared to manage grant opportunities.

During FY 2013, the Public Safety Communications Evolution Brochure was updated to help educate the public safety community and elected and appointed officials about the future of emergency communications, including the Nationwide Public Safety Broadband Network. The updated brochure describes the evolution of emergency communications and how traditional LMR communications used today may converge with wireless broadband in the future if specific requirements are met. The brochure also discusses some of the most important requirements that must be met to achieve the desired long-term state of convergence.

The FY 2013 SAFECOM Grant Guidance on Emergency Communications was also updated and released on February 25, 2013, providing guidance for state, local, and tribal grantees on eligible activities and equipment standards that may be applicable to Federal grants funding emergency communications projects. The scope of the SAFECOM guidance continues to expand beyond more traditional land mobile radio activities to encompass additional content on data, video, and other facets of broadband systems and other advanced technologies. OEC guidance documents are available on the _SAFECOM Program website_ for stakeholder use. The SAFECOM Program website is in the process of receiving updates in order to enhance the user experience.

- **Project 25 Compliance Assessment Program (P25 CAP)**

P25 CAP, established in coordination with NIST, provides an independent and transparent process to formally assess communications equipment against a select group of requirements within the suite of P25 CAP standards. P25 CAP provides first responders with a consistent resource for P25 compliance information, listing multiple vendors' products to support procurement decisions. This provides purchasers with increased confidence that the products being procured meet P25 CAP standards.

The SAFECOM Grant Guidance on Emergency Communications and FEMA's Grant Guidance encourages the purchase of P25 CAP compliant emergency communications equipment. This helps ensure Federal grant funds are going towards interoperable solutions for state, local, and tribal entities. Ultimately, this reduces potential waste due to the procurement of high cost proprietary equipment.

P25 CAP participating manufacturers represent over 90% of the P25 marketplace. In FY13, the OIC issued a Federal Register Notice to solicit expressions of interests from international accreditation bodies to become part of the P25 CAP. OIC received expressions of interest from three International Laboratory Accreditation Cooperation Full Member Mutual Recognition Arrangement Signatories. In FY14, the OIC will work with these entities to transition laboratory accreditation authorities within P25 CAP. This transition will result in a self-sustaining P25 CAP for the first responder community.

APPENDIX A: EXAMPLES OF AGENCY-SPECIFIC BENEFITS

Many E-Government initiatives and lines of business are funded through contributions made by partner agencies. In accordance with section 732(b)(1) of the Act, this appendix provides highlights of the benefits partner agencies receive through the initiatives and lines of business. This appendix does not include information on the benefits of initiatives which are funded by a single agency, as that information may be found above in the summaries of E-Government initiatives.

Budget Formulation and Execution Line of Business (BFE LoB)

Managing Partner: U.S. Department of Education

- **U.S. Department of Agriculture**

The BFE LoB provides USDA with a variety of budget tools, resources, and training opportunities which USDA utilizes to enhance communications and streamline processes. USDA employees are able to participate in training opportunities provided through the BFE LoB's Human Capital Federal Budget Core Competency Framework at no cost to the department. The relevance and quality of the material presented in the classes is highly regarded by USDA personnel.

USDA also utilizes the "MAX Federal Community," a secure government-only collaborative website, which provides collaboration across and within agencies, as well as knowledge management. USDA currently has approximately 2,500 users registered for the MAX Federal Community. The Community site can be used for sharing information, collaboratively drafting documents (including the direct-editing of documents posted on the site), supporting workgroups, submitting central reports, and much more.

Similarly, "MAX Collect" provides for the rapid collection and compilation of information for data calls from multiple sources - replacing the typical labor intensive process of manually compiling e-mailed word documents and spreadsheets. It enables the rapid structuring (within hours) of a custom tailored web-based data exercise that can collect both textual and numeric data, both unstructured and formatted, from tens or even hundreds of sources.

Finally, the Budgeting Capabilities Self-Assessment Tool (BCSAT) provides USDA budget managers and their staff with a simple survey-like method to assess and gain perspective on how their current operations and processes compare against best practices in a broad range of budgeting capability categories. This allows managers to strategically focus improvement efforts on areas of highest value to their particular organization's activities.

- **U.S. Department of Commerce**

DOC has benefited from a variety of resources provided through the BFE LoB. DOC utilizes the MAX Federal Community to share budget information with OMB and other Federal agencies, collaborate on internally and externally facing initiatives, and hold on-line meetings with remote participants. Many agencies within DOC use several MAX Collect exercises and associated publishing capabilities to collect, store, process and publish information from multiple sources in an efficient and effective manner, producing high quality output. The BFE LoB also provides DOC with increased analytical and reporting capability through the ongoing systems development, such as MAX Analytics. In addition, DOC utilizes the BCSAT to assess organizational practices and develop strategic plans addressing areas of need.

The BFE LoB also chartered a workgroup with the intent of reducing the need for duplicate data entry by agencies into the MAX A-11 system, and improving the quality of data and data exchange. DOC participated in the process of developing standard formats for data submission and rules validation, and working to coordinate agency efforts to build or update agency budget systems to interface with MAX A-11 directly. DOC also benefits from monthly BFE LoB panel discussions with senior agency and OMB experts, which cover insightful budget-related subjects.

DOC has also encouraged the use of the BFE LoB-developed self-paced training modules, addressing budget formulation, budget execution, and appropriations law. Approximately 2,200 DOC personnel benefited from training modules in FY 2013. These online, self- training modules have provided DOC budget professionals with a better understanding of Federal budgeting, and the importance of the role they play in the budget process.

- **U.S. Department of Defense**

DOD continues to contribute funds for the purpose of upgrading the MAX Apportionment System. This upgrade significantly eases DOD's workload in preparing and submitting apportionment requests to OMB. The process for agencies to prepare and submit apportionments is predicated upon the agency submitting a single request for a given Treasury Appropriation Fund Symbol (TAFS) and receiving approval from OMB prior to submitting additional requests for the same TAFS.

DOD is unique among agencies because of statutory requirements from congressional Appropriation Subcommittees that require DOD to prepare and submit two or more requests for a given TAFS at the same time. In addition to the difficulties involved in making multiple submissions within the current system and processes, when multiple requests process simultaneously the outcome is often that apportionments are overlaid with incorrect amounts and later require technical correction.

Upgrading the system allows DOD to use on-line screens to provide much of its requested data, avoiding providing data in Excel files, and enabling DOD to submit multiple apportionment requests on any given account, regardless of other unapproved apportionments still awaiting approval, while ensuring the outcome is correct. Upgrading the system facilitates informing OMB budget examiners as to which requests are higher priority than others, and facilitates integrating footnotes into the request. Additionally, the upgrade provides DOD with the ability to withdraw a request, and would allow DOD to receive notification when a request is denied by the examining division.

DOD also participates in the development of upgrades to the MAX A-11 system. These upgrades include improved schedule and line services, an account information viewer, modernizing the appendix text program, developing a Federal credit programs tool, and implementing various other shared services relating to MAX A-11.

- **U.S. Department of Energy**

DOE utilizes the Performance Measure Manager (PMM) as the centralized system of record for performance management within DOE. DOE uses the system to produce periodic reports for internal program management and OMB required reporting.

There are currently over 100 registered users utilizing the secure database with varying levels of responsibility. The web-based system is highly accessible for those entering and retrieving performance data, and the user-friendly interface facilitates ease of use. PMM is also accessible through the MAX system, and is customizable which allows the system to be modified to meet DOE's needs. In building the FY 2014 performance section of the DOE budget, PMM proved instrumental in combining and reducing the size of the report comparison to the previous fiscal year.

- **U.S. Department of Health and Human Services**

The HHS MAX Federal Community has over 5,500 registered users and continues to grow. The community site is commonly used for several purposes including information sharing, collaboratively drafting documents, and supporting workgroups.

The HHS Office of Budget uses MAX Community to collect annual budget justification materials from operating divisions across HHS. In addition, the Office of Budget has created a Budget Execution Training page on MAX Community, which includes video modules for receiving, controlling and distributing, spending, and accounting for resources, apportionments, executing a budget using an accounting system, and treasury warrants. It also includes examples of budget execution training documents. These videos and training documents are available to all HHS users across the various operating divisions.

The Budget Formulation and Execution Branch within the Office of Budget has also created a resource page for incoming budget analysts. This page provides information on the HHS organizational structure and internal resources, relevant legislation, general budgeting resources, formulation-specific guidance and products, execution-specific guidance, OMB budget data requests and guidance, and apportionment trainings.

HHS also uses MAX Community to support the Combined Federal Campaign (CFC), sharing information with CFC managers across operating and staff divisions, holding online meetings with remote participants, posting data requests, and collaborating with other agencies.

- **U.S. Department of Homeland Security**

The BFE LoB provides tools and resources to improve collaboration among the 15 components that comprise DHS. Through the BFE LoB, DHS was introduced to the Budget Formulation and Execution Manager (BFEM), the first shared service budget formulation system. The BFEM is used to produce the annual budget request, and has provided DHS with a cost-effective option for automating the development of the budget submission. The BFEM has also created a vehicle to potentially streamline the process for reconciling funding levels in the budget justification, and the MAX A-11 Data Entry application, a comprehensive tool for entering data required for the budget submission.

In addition, the BFE LoB has contributed to the improvement of DHS's use of the MAX Federal Community to collaborate on internal and external initiatives, and hold on-line meetings with remote participants in a cost-effective and efficient manner. With the support of the BFE LoB, DHS successfully implemented collaborative public safety initiatives with other Federal agencies to ensure continuity of operations using the MAX Federal Community and MAX Collect.

BFE LoB also has a workgroup with the intent of reducing the need for duplicate data entry by agencies into the MAX A-11 DE system by improving the quality of data and data exchange. DHS has participated in the process of developing standard formats for data submission and rules validation, and continues its work to coordinate agency efforts in securing a single sign-on capability. BFE LoB's workgroup developed a governmentwide directory page in the MAX Federal Community to help users identify their counterparts across the Federal government to discuss, collaborate, communicate, and share information. DHS employees can easily use the tools to add or update users, and modify the contact list as needed. DHS has also independently created several MAX Collect exercises and used the tool to gather, store, process and publish information from multiple sources in an extremely efficient manner. Additionally, DHS has used the self-paced training modules found on the Community which reduces personnel training costs.

- **U.S. Department of Housing and Urban Development**

HUD has participated in the process of developing standards formats for data submission and rules validation, and worked to coordinate agency efforts to build or update agency budget systems to interface with MAX A-11 directly. HUD continues to utilize the BCSAT to assess organizational practices and develop strategic plans addressing areas of need.

In addition, HUD currently has approximately 700 users registered for the MAX Federal Community. MAX Collect exercises have been created to support collection and publication ranging from creating portions of the annual budget request, to agency responses to Questions for the Record, to tracking Federal internet domain usage. The tool allows HUD to improve efficiency, meet assignments, and respond to data calls and questions more effectively and in a timely, even as they operate in a more restricted staffing environment. BFE LoB continues to be a corroborative and valuable mechanism during a financially difficult time, saving dollars through the use of the open standards MAX applications and avoiding duplicative use of government resources.

- **U.S. Department of the Interior**
The BFE LoB has benefitted DOI by leveraging the benefits of shared services for training, providing resources through the MAX Community, and providing centralized documentation. These critical services preserve DOI resources by reducing effort, cutting lead time, and maximizing collaboration.

DOI has had great success using the MAX Federal Community to monitor and streamline the QFR process. DOI has centralized the guidance and transmittal process by creating a common access point for critical documentation. Doing so has reduced email traffic and created a central repository for deliverables. Bureaus and departmental staff can also work together to finalize documentation to be transmitted to leadership, reducing the number of versions being worked at once and improving collaboration. DOI has also made use of the shared workspace, and has created pages for finalizing and submitting budget justifications materials, which reduces review time and effort for DOI.

DOI has also leveraged the BFE LoB documentation and centralized training to expand the knowledge base of DOI employees. Specifically, DOI has benefited from the BFE LoB Decision Matrix, a tool which compares all budget systems' ratings and capabilities, and provides summary and detailed information on each system. The BFE LoB Decision Matrix has been a particularly useful tool for developing a base set of requirements for a budget formulation system. DOI employees have also benefitted from BFE LoB sponsored training classes for government budget community, and online, self-paced modules which cover topics such as Federal appropriations law, budget formulation and execution, how to balance a MAX account, Federal credit, and budget reduction.

- **U.S. Department of Justice**
DOJ's central budget office has been very successful in implementing MAX Collect capabilities, and has been approached by many DOJ components and senior leadership offices to develop new Collect exercises to increase efficiencies, streamline work processes, and improve workflow processes. DOJ continues to be at the forefront of exploring new ways to utilize these capabilities. DOJ transitioned from its aging performance system to a new MAX Collect application.

DOJ also continues to explore new ways in which MAX Analytics capabilities can be used to enhance the use of MAX Collect. The BFE LoB has worked with DOJ to provide increased analytical and reporting capability through ongoing systems development resulting in additional MAX Collect/Analytics capabilities, which allowed DOJ to move forward in transitioning the current crosscut process into a MAX Collect exercise. DOJ continues to utilize MAX Collect for the QFR process, which was enhanced this year by the new reporting capabilities in MAX Collect. DOJ successfully partnered with other agencies to co-fund improvements to MAX Analytics, providing DOJ, as well as all BFE LoB partner agencies, with significant upgrades to MAX analytics capabilities.

In FY 2013, DOJ began providing DOJ users the ability to use single sign on capability to access the MAX Community, MAX A-11 database, and DOJ's budget formulation system. This capability was very well received by DOJ users, improving access time and negating the need to remember numerous passwords. Finally, DOJ utilizes the BFE LoB developed self-paced training modules pertaining to budget formulation and execution, appropriations law, basic budget concepts, and reductions for staff training. DOJ has incorporated these modules into the new employee orientation process, making them required training for new budget analysts.

- **U.S. Department of Labor**

DOL uses the MAX Community to post published budgets and transmittal memorandums, allowing DOL personnel to download, evaluate and comment prior to OMB Passback. In addition, the availability of the Human Capital Solution workgroup's online courses have offered direct benefit to new DOL personnel by reducing the on-boarding process, and creating consistency in budget vernacular. DOL personnel also benefit from the forums organized by the BFE LoB, which bring together the budgeting and program analyst communities. These forums open up dialogue, increase transparency and drive information sharing not otherwise available. During these forums, analysts from across the government can meet with panelists and discuss a multitude of budget topics. In addition, these forums offer an opportunity for the communities to learn about recent BFE LoB accomplishments, and the program's future roadmap.

- **U.S. Department of State**

State participates with the MAX Federal Community, and uses the tool to share budget information with their own departments and other Federal agencies, collaborate on internally and externally-facing initiatives, and hold on-line meetings with remote participants. Additionally, the BCSAT has provided State with a simple survey-like method to assess and gain perspective on how current operations and processes compare against best practices in a broad range of budgeting capability categories. State has reviewed how to use the BCSAT to assess organizational practices and develop strategic plans to address areas of need. State also utilizes the BFE LoB self-paced training modules for beginning and mid-level staff training, and has incorporated the modules into the Bureau of Budget and Planning's formal training plan.

- **U.S. Department of Transportation**

DOT utilizes the tools and services provided by the BFE LoB to improve efficiency and effectiveness in formulating and executing DOT budgets. The BFE LoB provides central integration and standardized exchange of budget formulation, execution, planning, performance measurement, and financial management information. The BFE LoB also provides capabilities for analyzing data in support of decision-making, and capabilities for aligning programs to institutionalize budget and performance integration. In addition, DOT has improved efficiency through the use of the MAX Collect site. DOT utilizes the data collection capabilities of MAX Collect, and the ability for users to receive email notifications of new budget data calls and exercises. Finally, the BFE LoB has benefitted DOT by leveraging shared services for training, the MAX Community, and centralized documentation. These critical services preserve DOT resources by reducing effort, cutting lead time, and maximizing collaboration.

- **U.S. Department of the Treasury**

Treasury participated in the BFE LoB process of developing standard formats for data submission and rules validation, and worked to coordinate agency efforts to build or update agency budget system to interface with MAX A-11 directly. Treasury also encouraged the use of the BFE LoB-developed self-paced training modules for staff training. Approximately 3,200 Treasury personnel benefited from this training in FY 2013.

- **U.S. Department of Veterans Affairs**

The VA supports the BFE LoB cross-governmental efforts to reduce duplicative data entry requirements with MAX A-11 system. The VA uses the MAX Federal Community to share budget information and collaborate with OMB. The VA also uses MAX Collect to fulfill many OMB requests for data. The VA supports the continued work of the BFE LoB and views the initiative as a central clearing house for improvements in budget formulation, execution, audit and professional development.

- **U.S. Agency for International Development**

USAID has realized a number of benefits as a result of participating in the BFE LoB. USAID uses the MAX Federal Community, which provides a collaborative workspace that facilitates transparency, effective data mining, and improved access to critical documentation. USAID has also leveraged BFE LoB documentation and centralized training to expand the knowledge base of USAID employees. The USAID Budget Analyst Roundtable in particular has taken advantage of the training offered by the BFE LoB. Looking ahead, USAID is examining the possibility of using MAX Collect for internal budget execution exercises.

- **U.S. Army Corps of Engineers**

USACE personnel benefit from the budget-related training offered through the BFE LoB. In addition, USACE's objective is to have access to systems, programs, and secure web-links developed by BFE LoB for budget-related expertise, tools and services that enhance budgeting analysis, document production, data collection and tracking and secure collaboration and on line meetings. USACE has also benefited from using the MAX Community to respond to budget data requests (BDR) more efficiently and effectively, as well as using the tool for data collection and tracking. USACE now uses the MAX Collect tool to respond to 100% of BDR's. The tool is faster and more effective in that it eliminates e-mails, has no file size restrictions, and there are no firewalls between USACE, their program offices, and OMB.

- **Environmental Protection Agency**

EPA has benefitted from BFE LoB through information sharing from other agencies on various budget systems, and utilizing software provided through the initiative. The BFE LoB provides EPA with increased analytical and reporting capability through ongoing system development, such as MAX Analytics. The BFE LoB is also working to give EPA and other agencies the capability to have secure, virtual on-line meetings where participants can not only hear what's been said by conferencing into the meeting, but also view budget-related presentations directly from their workspace. In addition, the BFE LoB has provided budget-related training to the EPA budget employees on OMB's MAX budget system, training on how Treasury's FACTS II statements tie into the budget process, refresher training on the basic principles of budgeting, and the "Warrants and Apportionments" webinar where subject matter experts from OMB delivered an overview of, as well as, tips and tricks on the apportionment process. EPA has also provided support to the training efforts of the BFE LoB. EPA managers have served as mentors to Federal government employees during the "Speed Mentoring" sessions held at the Department of Education.

- **General Services Administration**

GSA participates in the BFE LoB task force, which is made up of agency representatives and meets regularly, both in person and on-line. The task force identifies opportunities for common budgeting solutions, as well as automated tools to augment the agency budget process. GSA also utilizes the BFE LoB MAX calendar for agency and individual use. The MAX calendar is a web-based calendaring application that facilitates cross-agency meetings by providing a central location for MAX users to share their 'free/busy' information with selected users and groups. Finally, GSA benefits from the various training sessions available through BFE LoB, including "Exploring Basic Budget Processes," and "Appropriations Law."

- **National Aeronautics and Space Administration**

The BFE LoB provides significant benefits to NASA by encouraging best practices crossing all aspects of Federal budgeting. NASA currently has its own budgeting tools, and has not chosen to move to a new budget system. However NASA is exploring using a shared service budget system moving forward. NASA does, however, utilize the BFE LoB MAX Federal Community, which provides significant benefits for collaboration across and within agencies, as well as knowledge management. The Community site is commonly used for sharing information, and collaboratively drafting documents, including directly editing documents posted on the site.

- **National Science Foundation**

NSF often utilizes the MAX Federal Community as an externally-facing collaboration vehicle for such activities as responding to OMB data calls, and receiving budget guidance from OMB and other federal agencies. The MAX Federal Community page provides NSF with an automated system for ensuring data and information are transmitted in a clear and consistent manner as required by the budget data calls. In addition, NSF staff routinely use the BFE LoB-developed self-paced training modules on budgetary concepts for staff training. Training topics offered through the MAX Community page and utilized by NSF staff include appropriations law, budget formulation, and budget execution.

- **Office of National Drug Control Policy**

ONDCP uses the MAX Collect system as the mechanism to capture information from agencies that support the implementation of the *National Drug Control Strategy*. Since the MAX Collect system is internet-accessible, lead agencies can update information on an ongoing basis, and ONDCP can review input and monitor progress in real-time. Based upon the successful use of the MAX system to oversee the implementation of the National Drug Control Strategy, MAX Collect is being used to coordinate implementation of the Administration's *Prescription Drug Abuse Prevention Plan* and *National Northern Border Counternarcotics Strategy* and will soon include the *2013 National Southwest Border Counternarcotics Strategy*. In addition, ONDCP and its Delivery Unit use the MAX Community to house the ONDCP Strategic Priorities Database. Internal performance is tracked for end of year reporting to senior ONDCP officials.

- **Office of Personnel Management**

OPM benefited from several BFE LoB investments in FY 2013. MAX Collect enables OPM to efficiently provide input to Governmentwide reporting, with a verifiable audit trail in formats that are useful to the end user. The availability of MAX Collect to multiple users within OPM and the automated approval process has also enabled OPM to decentralize some of this reporting.

The enhancements to the automated apportionment system developed by the BFE LoB permit OPM to create accurate, complete apportionment documents and document the approval process at both OPM and at OMB. The tool also provides an archive of prior apportionments. The consistent formatting required by the tool enables comparison with periodic Reports on Budget Execution and Budgetary Resources filed via the Financial Management Service's FACTS-II system.

OPM made extensive use of the web-based MAX data entry piloted during preparation of the FY 2014 President's Budget. It enabled OPM staff to enter, diagnose and submit account data from remote locations via a browser based application. The enhanced error reporting and resolution capabilities made the process more efficient. OPM anticipates that new archive capabilities will help with presentation of the 2015 President's Budget. Finally, the document repository within the MAX Federal Community provides OPM and others with a convenient one-stop reference site for frequently used material.

- **Securities and Exchange Commission**

Through the BFE LoB, SEC personnel have participated in workgroups, such as the 2013 Spring Forum, that explored specific aspects of Federal Budgeting and how they could benefit from improved processes and tools. SEC personnel benefitted from helping to develop common solutions, and sharing lessons learned and best practices across agencies through meetings and information sharing with budget colleagues.

The SEC has also benefitted from the MAX Federal Community through its interagency collaboration and knowledge management service. At any given time during the year, SEC personnel use the online community to gather information, and share with colleagues on topics pertaining to financial management, small agency performance reporting, budget analytics, and E-Gov. Additionally, early career and senior staff have participated in several free, web-based, multi-media training courses for beginning or mid-level budget analysts, as well as monthly budget brown bags with senior agency and OMB experts, intended to provide varying levels of training and understanding of budget formulation and execution. The courses and monthly panel discussions have proven to be very beneficial method of training staff and keeping them abreast of best practices in the budget community.

In addition, the SEC has benefitted from MAX Collect, and its capability for the rapid collection and compiling of information. The workflow management capabilities allow staff to keep track of pending submissions and confirm and verify past submissions. Finally, the SEC was appreciative of the efforts made by BFE LoB to consolidate information on budget systems used governmentwide by Federal Shared Service Providers (FPPS) as the SEC contemplates possibilities for upgrading its current budget system or acquiring a new system. A key document called "The Decision Matrix" assisted the SEC as it reviewed several FPPS budget systems, and the BFE LoB facilitated contacts with those providers.

- **Small Business Administration**

The BFELoB provides benefits to SBA by encouraging best practices crossing all aspects of Federal budgeting. The SBA uses the MAX Federal Community to share budget information and collaborate with OMB. The SBA also uses MAX Collect to fulfill many OMB requests for data.

Disaster Assistance Improvement Program (DAIP)

Managing Partner: U.S. Department of Homeland Security

- **U.S. Department of Agriculture**

DAIP benefits USDA by providing stakeholders referrals to, and information on, 16 Federal forms of assistance (FOA's) related to food assistance, business loans, farm loans, and more. DAIP's outreach and education efforts help raise awareness of these FOA's among stakeholders at the Federal, state, local, and tribal levels. For example, USDA has deployed an interface with the *Food for Florida Disaster Supplemental Nutrition Assistance Program*, the first state-based interface in the DAIP portfolio. In addition, through *www.DisasterAssistance.gov*, USDA has recorded the following site usage metrics:

- 934,062 FOA page views;

- 76,938 transfers to USDA's domain; and,

- 26,912 referrals received from the questionnaire to the USDA FOA registration site.

DAIP also provides cost-savings related to decreased labor hours, automated tracking, reduced waste, fraud and abuse, and information-sharing, all of which help USDA assist disaster survivors more effectively. These savings will almost certainly grow in relative proportion to the growth of the portal and interface developments.

- **U.S. Department of Commerce**

While some agencies are affected less than others in times of a disaster, all are affected in some way. It is imperative that all agencies work together to assist agencies and individuals in need of assistance. This will help to ensure that DOC's non-disaster-specific assistance programs and services continue to reach disaster survivors who may be displaced or are otherwise out of contact. Active involvement in DAIP will also help reduce the burden on Federal agencies which routinely provide logistical help and other critical management or organizational support during disasters, even if those agencies do not provide individual assistance programs. Participation in DAIP provides a platform to offer application intake in the event that an agency Federal Forms of Assistance is authorized as a result of a disaster. It also offers a resource to individuals who inquire with the agency about disaster assistance.

- **U.S. Department of Education**

DAIP benefits ED by providing an interface on *www.DisasterAssistance.gov* for individuals to access their student loan and grant data. DAIP's outreach and education efforts help raise awareness of this FOA among the agency's stakeholders at the Federal, tribal, state and local levels. DAIP provides a range of metrics to ED each month to help illustrate the value of ED's partnership, and provide insight into survivor inquiry activity with respect to FOA's. Through *www.DisasterAssistance.gov*, ED has recorded the following site usage metrics between October 1, 2012 and August 31, 2013:

- 83,027 ED FOA page views;

- 10,164 exchanges of agency data to and from the interface;

- 7,808 referrals from the questionnaire to ED FOAs that transferred into the site's registration process;

- 2,770 transfers to ED's domain; and,

- 567 links from ED's domain to *www.DisasterAssistance.gov*.

- **U.S. Department of Health and Human Services**

DAIP benefits HHS by providing referrals to and information on FOA's, including the *Temporary Assistance for Needy Families* program and crisis counseling assistance, both of which can be of great help to disaster survivors. DAIP's outreach and education efforts also help to raise awareness of HHS FOA's among the agency's stakeholders at the Federal, state, local, and tribal levels. In addition, through *www.DisasterAssistance.gov*, HHS has recorded the following site usage metrics between October 1, 2012 and August 31, 2013:

- 1,147,240 HHS FOA page views;

- 36,336 referrals from the questionnaire to HHS FOAs that transferred into the site's registration process;

- 18,666 transfers to HHS' domain; and,

- 479 links from HHS' domain to *www.DisasterAssistance.gov*.

- **U.S. Department of Housing and Urban Development**

DAIP benefits HUD and its stakeholders by providing referrals to and information on FOAs related to housing assistance, including a program to help disaster survivors obtain mortgages to purchase or repair their homes. DAIP's outreach and education efforts also help to raise awareness of these FOA's among HUD's stakeholders at the Federal, state, local, and tribal levels. In addition, through *www.DisasterAssistance.gov*, HUD has recorded the following site usage metrics were reported between October 1, 2012 and August 31, 2013:

- 994,927 HUD FOA page views;

- 3,452 referrals from the questionnaire to HUD FOAs that transferred into the site's registration process;

- 2,835 links from HUD's domain to *www.DisasterAssistance.gov*; and,

- 2,127 transfers to HUD's domain.

To increase efficiencies, HUD and DAIP are collaboratively developing an interface whereby data can flow seamlessly and securely between HUD and FEMA. The interface will enable validations to determine whether or not HUD applicants have already received benefits through similar FEMA programs. The interface will help streamline the assistance application process for survivors, and also increase data security and reduce fraud, waste, abuse and redundancy.

- **U.S. Department of the Interior**

DAIP benefits DOI and its stakeholders by providing referrals to, and information on, the agency's *Bureau of Indian Affairs Financial Assistance and Social Services* program. DAIP officials have participated on the monthly Tribal Assistance Coordination Group conference calls, and provide information about *www.DisasterAssistance.gov* to share with tribes. These monthly calls have demonstrated DOI's commitment to assisting tribal nation's during disasters by allowing tribal leaders to speak directly with a number of Federal officials. The calls resulted in aid being provided to the tribes expeditiously. Calls are also held directly after a disaster to address emergency needs for both short and long term recovery, and assist the Bureau of Indian Affairs in raising the awareness of the DAIP program, so that DOI can share this information with tribal officials. In addition, through *www.DisasterAssistance.gov*, DOI has recorded the following site usage metrics between October 1, 2012 and August 31, 2013:

- 7,960 DOI FOA page views;

- 1,035 transfers to DOI's domain;

- 475 referrals from the questionnaire to DOI FOAs that transferred into the site's registration process; and,

- 238 links from DOI's domain to *www.DisasterAssistance.gov*.

- **U.S. Department of Justice**

DAIP benefits DOJ and its stakeholders by providing referrals to and information on three agency FOA's. The *Public Safety Officers' Benefits* program provides death benefit to the eligible survivors of Federal, state or local public safety officers whose death is the direct and proximate result of a personal injury sustained in the line of duty. The State Crime Victims Compensation program reimburses victims for crime-related expenses such as medical costs, mental health counseling, funeral and burial costs and lost wages or loss of support. Finally, the *International Terrorism Victim Expense Reimbursement* program reimburses eligible direct victims of designated acts of international terrorism that occur outside of the United States for expenses associated with the victimization. DAIP's outreach and education efforts also help to raise awareness of these FOA's among the agency's stakeholders at the Federal, tribal, state and local levels. In addition, through *www.DisasterAssistance.gov*, DOJ has recorded the following site usage metrics:

- 16,764 DOJ FOA page views;

- 1,133 referrals from the questionnaire to DOJ FOAs that transferred into the site's registration process;

- 659 transfers to DOJ's domain; and,

- 48 links from DOJ's domain to *www.DisasterAssistance.gov*.

- **U.S. Department of Labor**

DAIP serves DOL and its stakeholders by providing referrals to, and information on, three agency FOA's related to income and employment assistance, including disaster unemployment insurance. DAIP's outreach and education efforts also help to raise awareness of these FOA's among DOL stakeholders. In addition, through *www.DisasterAssistance.gov*, DOI has recorded the following site usage metrics between October 1, 2012 and August 31, 2013:

- 164,976 DOL FOA page views;

- 15,855 transfers from DOL's domain;

- 4,351 links from DOL's domain to *www.DisasterAssistance.gov*; and

- 3,917 referrals from the questionnaire to DOL FOAs that transferred into the site's registration process.

- ## U.S. Department of State

State participates in DAIP to help ensure that information on foreign disaster assistance and non-disaster-specific assistance programs and services continue to reach survivors who may be displaced or are otherwise out of contact. DAIP currently has a separate page on *www.DisasterAssistance.gov*, for information on foreign disasters to assist a survivor if they are in a foreign country. Continued active involvement in DAIP will also help reduce the burden on federal agencies which routinely provide logistical help and other critical management or organizational support during disasters, even if those agencies do not provide individual assistance programs. Participation in DAIP also provides a platform which offers application intake in the event that an agency FOA is authorized as a result of a disaster. It also acts as a resource for individuals inquiring about disaster assistance.

- ## U.S. Department of the Treasury

DAIP benefits Treasury and its stakeholders by providing referrals to, and information on, three FOA's that provide tax counseling and assistance to those whose property has been damaged or lost in a disaster, allow survivors to continue to receive federal benefit payments via a direct deposit program, and allow disaster survivors to expedite the replacement of missing savings bonds. In addition, through *www.DisasterAssistance.gov*, Treasury has recorded the following site usage metrics between October 1, 2012 and August 31, 2013:

- 819,541 Treasury FOA page views;

- 36,313 referrals from the questionnaire to Treasury FOAs that transferred into the site's registration process;

- 6,089 links to Treasury's domain; and,

- 4,423 transfers from Treasury's domain to *www.DisasterAssistance.gov*.

- ## U.S. Department of Veterans Affairs

DAIP benefits VA and its stakeholders by providing referrals to, and information on, eight FOA's that assist veterans with a range of needs, including health care, burial benefits, and change of address for benefits receipt. DAIP's outreach and education efforts also help to raise awareness of these FOA's among VA stakeholders. In addition, through *www.DisasterAssistance.gov*, Treasury has recorded the following site usage metrics between October 1, 2012 and August 31, 2013:

- 65,969 VA FOA page views;

- 2,955 referrals from the questionnaire to VA FOAs that transferred into the site's registration process;

- 627 transfers to VA's domain; and,

- 142 links from VA's domain to www.DisasterAssistance.gov.

- **Office of Personnel Management**

DAIP benefits OPM and its stakeholders by providing a referral to and information on the agency's federal retiree benefits program, which provides retired and retirement- eligible federal employees with an online means to access and modify personal information about their benefits and annuity payments. In addition, through *www.DisasterAssistance.gov*, OPM has recorded the following site usage metrics between October 1, 2012 and August 31, 2013:

  - 5,145 OPM FOA page views;

  - 556 referrals from the questionnaire to OPM FOAs that transferred into the site's registration process; and,

  - 225 transfers to OPM's domain.

- **Small Business Administration**

Before the development of DAIP, SBA and FEMA had an existing, longstanding partnership when dealing with disaster recovery efforts. The agencies have had an interface between information technology systems for over 16 years, and DAIP has worked to improve the partnership allowing for the improved use of technology in the interfaces, enhanced data integrity, reduction of errors and improvement of service to disaster survivors.

DisasterAssistance.gov serves SBA and its stakeholders by providing referrals to, and information on, two agency FOA's that provide financial assistance to businesses, non-profit organizations, homeowners and renters whose property has been damaged by a disaster. DAIP's outreach and education efforts help to raise awareness of these FOAs among the agency's stakeholders at the Federal, state, local, and tribal levels.

DisasterAssistance.gov also links to the SBA Electronic Loan Application Portal whereby survivors can submit their name and address information directly to the SBA Disaster Credit Management System. This provides the survivor with a "no-wrong-door" approach to applying for disaster loan assistance. Additionally, DAIP will provide loan packets to applicants also applying for FEMA assistance which eliminates the need for survivors to place a separate call or inquiry to SBA in order to receive the loan packets and information.

Finally, through *www.DisasterAssistance.gov*, SBA has recorded the following site usage metrics between October 1, 2012 and August 31, 2013:

- 1,289,904 exchanges of agency data to and from the interface;

- 674,768 SBA FOA page views;

- 35,857 referrals from the questionnaire to SBA FOAs that transferred into the site's registration process;

- 31,108 links from SBA's domain to *www.DisasterAssistance.gov*; and,

- 3,032 transfers to SBA's domain.

- **Social Security Administration**

DAIP benefits SSA and its stakeholders by providing referrals to, and information on, Social Security, disability, Medicare and other benefits/information. DAIP's outreach and education efforts also help to raise awareness of this assistance among the agency's stakeholders at the Federal, state, local, and tribal levels. For example, DAIP and SSA developed an interface whereby users can change their Social Security benefit delivery addresses directly through _www.DisasterAssistance.gov_. This streamlined service, which is provided through the same application as other agency assistance programs, helps get much needed income into the hands of displaced disaster survivors. Additionally, through _www._ _DisasterAssistance.gov_ SSA has recorded the following site usage metrics between October 1, 2012 and August 31, 2013:

- 266,641 SSA FOA page views;

- 7,345 referrals from the questionnaire to SSA FOAs that transferred into the site's registration process;

- 3,602 exchanges of agency data to and from the interface;

- 2,127 transfers to SSA's domain; and,

- 266 links from SSA's domain to _www.DisasterAssistance.gov_.

Federal Health Architecture Line of Business (FHA LoB)

Managing Partner: U.S. Department of Health and Human Services

- **U.S. Department of Defense**

DOD utilizes the FHA LoB to assist Service members as they transition to Veterans status and the VA health system. The delivery of services and benefits is enhanced through real-time electronic access to health information, and ensures the security and privacy of personal information across DOD. In 2013, DOD began integrating a FHA LoB-developed enhancement to the eHealth Exchange CONNECT software into the Virtual Lifetime Electronic Record (VLER) Health Exchange baseline. The software enhancements will enable DOD to securely review authorizations to release medical information signed by claimants seeking SSA disability benefits. DOD will then be able to use the eHealth Exchange to provide SSA State Disability Determination Services with nearly real-time access to protected health information (PHI) and personally identifiable information (PII). In FY 2014, DOD will invest an additional $562,000 for CONNECT software development.

By making the flow of health information more efficient, VLER supports the potential reduction in duplication of effort that occurs when a patient receives care at multiple facilities, which may free up valuable resources, equipment, and staff that would otherwise be needed to perform duplicative tests. In addition, the FHA DIRECT project provides a secure, point-to-point information exchange that can be leveraged to transmit PHI and PII. In 2013, DOD piloted the DIRECT information exchange standards and services with a private sector health care organization. The pilot demonstrated that DIRECT could be adapted to meet DOD security and privacy policies for exchanging sensitive health information with TRICARE Network Providers. DOD will evaluate the DIRECT post-pilot evaluation report to determine next steps.

- **U.S. Department of Veterans Affairs**

Data for veterans who have opted to share their health data and are enrolled in the VA Health Care system is accessible to 117,500 VA clinicians as well as eHealth Exchange participating private sector health care providers and specialists. VA clinicians have benefitted from faster system response times when requesting patient data from private sector providers, and also by having a larger amount of Veterans' health data accessible to them. At the beginning of FY 2013, the average response time from when a user initiated a query until the data is displayed was 2 minutes. This response time has been reduced to an average of 25 seconds, representing an 80% improvement in response time.

In addition, the VA utilizes the CONNECT software provided through the FHA LoB. VA is able to adapt the software to draw health information from VA's central data store, and format the information according to national standards for retrieval by private sector health exchange partners and health care providers.

- **Social Security Administration**

SSA utilizes health IT to drive down costs and speed up determination processes by making it possible to more quickly evaluate healthcare records of individuals with disabilities and distribute benefits more efficiently. Obtaining medical records electronically plays a key role in streamlining the disability determination process.

SSA's Medical Evidence Gathering and Analysis through the Health IT (MEGAHIT) project is migrating the healthcare documentation process from paper-based to electronic format. Automating the request and receipt of medical evidence reduces administrative costs of paper handling and associated costs of mailing, scanning, and printing paper records. It also enables faster disability determinations, providing patients with faster access to Medicare or Medicaid benefits, improved patient satisfaction, and automated payments from Social Security. For example, MedVirginia has assisted in over 13,000 disability determinations and cut almost in half the time it typically takes to get through the process. Overall, utilizing health IT has resulted in a 14%, or 13 days reduction in initial case processing time, which previously averaged 90 days.

In FY 2013, SSA expanded to 20 active health IT partners. These partnerships provide SSA with access to numerous medical sources in 19 states and the District of Columbia. SSA will continue expanding to additional facilities with current eHealth Exchange partners, and add new organizations each year.

Financial Management Line of Business (FM LoB)

Managing Partner: U.S. Department of the Treasury

- **U.S. Department of Agriculture**

The FM LoB provides USDA with standards, requirements, tools, and services to support USDA's financial management activities. USDA benefits from information shared across the Federal community pertaining to standards and best practices in implementing financial systems, and commercial software products used across government.

FM LoB supports the modernization of USDA financial systems. This support has allowed USDA to continue the implementation of an integrated financial system, providing USDA with a detailed and unified view of agency operations. In FY 2013, USDA continued deployment of the Financial Management Modernization Initiative (FMMI), a new financial system that replaces USDA's legacy financial system. FMMI is based upon a commercial, off-the-shelf resource planning product. FMMI is an advanced, web-based, financial management system that provides general accounting, funds management, and financial-reporting capabilities that has been deployed to 28 of USDA's 29 administrative organizations. In addition to utilizing the product, USDA also chairs the Customer Control Board to exchange information, and ensure that future product releases and enhancements are aligned with Federal standards.

In addition, FM LoB coordinates several financial management and financial services transparency efforts including the Central Contractor Registry, the Data Universal Numbering System, USASpending.gov and sub-recipient reporting, all of which improve the efficiency and effectiveness of these systems for USDA users. In FY 2013, the FM LoB managing partner worked diligently to address issues with the System for Award Management platform, which should restore stability and efficiency for USDA and its stakeholders. Automation of the verification process could help to minimize the administrative burden on the contracting, procurement and grant communities by reducing the amount of time it takes to verify eligibility. Websites like _www.USASpending.gov_ also allow USDA to inform the public on how tax payer dollars for Federal financial assistance and contracts are spent, and remain compliant with legal requirements and OMB guidelines.

- **U.S. Department of Commerce**

DOC leverages the FM LoB to reduce costs, and implement and operate financial management systems through a standardized system and business processes. These efforts will bridge the gap between DOC and the Federal financial management community. DOC realizes cost savings through FM LoB's efforts to transform Federal management through the reduction of duplicate efforts. The evaluation of all new agency systems modernizations plans, core governmentwide financial requirements, and facilitation of the implementation of governmentwide operational capabilities will assist DOC in reducing costs and increasing transparency department-wide.

DOC's contributions to the FM LoB will help to provide improved solutions for the financial management community, including financial assistance program management and reporting, and enhanced alignment among the financial assistance communities. The FM LoB also enables DOC to improve reporting of Federal spending to various stakeholders, including Congress and the general public, by improving the consistency and quality of data.

- ## U.S. Department of Defense

DOD's contributions to the FM LoB will help to provide improved solutions for the financial management community, including financial assistance program management and reporting, while also enhancing alignment among the financial assistance communities. This will benefit all funding bureaus, DOD, and the overall financial management community. FM LoB will enable the DoD to improve reporting transparency of Federal spending to stakeholders including Congress and the public. FM LoB will improve the consistency and quality of data across all financial spending communities including acquisitions and financial assistance. The efforts of the FM LoB include saving taxpayer dollars, improving public reporting of DOD financial data, reducing administrative burdens, reducing the risk of waste, fraud, and abuse, while significantly improving financial management services within DOD.

- ## U.S. Department of Education

The Department of the Treasury's Office of Financial Innovation and Transformation (FIT) is working with ED to ensure that the department is positioned to adopt a shared service approach. FIT will work with ED to evaluate any new agency systems modernizations plans and requirements, and maintain core governmentwide financial requirements while limiting expansion and impact on financial system requirements. FIT will assist ED in identifying and facilitating the implementation of operational capabilities such as invoice processing and centralized receivables management, helping reduce costs and increase transparency.

- ## U.S. Department of Energy

Treasury is working with the DOE to analyze opportunities to benefit from shared services. DOE is on target to implement mandates that help improve governmentwide operational capabilities. For example, DOE is on schedule to implement procedures to reconcile its financial system with _www.USASpending.gov_, thereby ensuring DOE is providing current and accurate information to the general public. Additionally, DOE has worked diligently with Treasury to accommodate the new Governmentwide Treasury Account Symbol Adjusted Trial Balance System (GTAS). GTAS is a web-based systems implemented to merge the functionality of four current stovepipe applications that collect trial balance data. Consolidating systems facilitates data consistency checks, and reduced maintenance and reporting costs. Consolidation also allows agencies to submit proprietary and budgetary data simultaneously in one submission, saving users time and avoiding the need to use two separate systems.

- ## U.S. Department of Health and Human Services

HHS supports the FM LoB, and plans to continue working collaboratively with the FM LoB to facilitate strong financial and grant management processes and associated cross-government initiatives. Ultimately, HHS's contributions to the FM LoB will help to provide improved solutions for the financial management community including financial assistance program management and reporting, and enhanced alignment among the financial assistance communities. The FM LoB will also enable HHS to improve reporting transparency of Federal spending to stakeholders including the Congress and the public, by improving the consistency and quality of HHS data across all financial spending communities including acquisitions and financial assistance.

- **U.S. Department of Homeland Security**

The FM LoB is responsible for cross-agency financial management transparency solutions including the System of Management (SAM), the Data Universal Numbering System (DUNS), *www.USASpending. gov*, and sub-recipient reporting. These solutions help DHS streamline financial management and assistance business processes, and data management practices. For example, SAM consolidates records from the legacy Central Contractor Registry solution, the Online Representations and Certifications Application, and exclusion records from the Excluded Parties List System into one website. This increases efficiency and makes it easier to obtain information.

The FM LoB also established a program management infrastructure, enabling DHS to participate in the initiative. The FM LoB conducts planning activities on behalf of all partner agencies, including the establishment of Memorandums of Understanding (MOU's) with partner agencies, coordination with OMB, and engagement with key stakeholders.

Ultimately, DHS's contributions will help provide improved solutions for the financial management community including financial assistance program management and reporting, and enhanced alignment among the financial assistance communities. This will benefit all funding bureaus within DHS, and the overall financial management community. Finally, the FM LoB enables DHS to improve reporting transparency of Federal spending to stakeholders including Congress and the public. The FM LoB improves the consistency and quality of DHS data across all financial spending communities including acquisitions and financial assistance.

- **U.S. Department of Housing and Urban Development**

The FM LoB will enable HUD to improve reporting transparency of Federal spending to stakeholders including Congress and the public. The FM LoB will improve the consistency and quality of HUD data across all financial spending areas, including acquisitions and financial assistance.

- **U.S. Department of the Interior**

The FM LoB supports DOI's efforts to save taxpayer dollars, improve public reporting of Federal financial data, reduce administrative burdens, reduce the risk of waste, fraud, and abuse, and significantly improve financial management services across the Government. DOI's contribution to the FM LoB supports efforts to standardize, optimize, and consolidate agency financial systems that will decrease system redundancy while driving cost-savings through development, modernization, and enhancement, as well as operations and maintenance cost reductions and data standardization. DOI has established a MOU with Treasury to further support coordination with key stakeholders, as well as improved its efforts to promote transparency of Federal spending and improved agency operations.

- ## U.S. Department of Justice

Treasury's responsibility over other cross-agency financial management transparency solutions, including the Central Contractor Registry, the Data Universal Numbering System, _www.USASpending.gov_, and sub-recipient reporting, will help DOJ streamline financial management, and provide assistance with business processes and data management practices.

The FM LoB program management infrastructure enables DOJ to easily participate in the initiative. DOJ benefits from the FM LoB planning activities conducted on behalf of all partner agencies, including establishment of memorandums of understanding, coordination with OMB, and engagement with key stakeholders. The FM LoB also enables Justice to improve reporting transparency of Federal spending to stakeholders, including Congress and the public. FM LoB will improve the consistency and quality of data across all financial spending communities, including acquisitions and financial assistance. Ultimately, DOJ contributions will help to provide improved solutions for the financial management community.

- ## U.S. Department of Labor

The FM LoB funds activities under the Council on Financial Assistance Reform (COFAR). The COFAR is charged to develop policies and take actions to improve grants administration through identification of emerging issues, challenges, and opportunities in grants management and providing recommendations to OMB. As one of the eight largest grant making agencies, DOL is a permanent member and contributor to the COFAR. DOL is a direct beneficiary of its contribution to the FM LoB through its seat on the COFAR, which enables DOL to directly influence the direction, flow and activities undertaken. In FY 2014, COFAR will publish a guidance document addressing administrative requirement, cost principles, and audit requirements for Federal awards. This guidance document is the culmination of two years' work, and combines eight guidance documents into one.

In addition, the FM LoB provides public, validated financial data that aligns spending information with core financial accounting data. DOL has examined its workflow process related to its submission of grants data to USASpending, and has developed procedures to identify and correct data errors. Further, to improve data quality reported to USASpending, DOL will compare the unique Federal Award Identification Number to corresponding data in the core financial management system. Finally, DOL has also reduced the number of unclean audit opinions for grant recipients. DOL has used the Federal Audit Clearinghouse submission data to identify governmentwide trends in deficiencies, and establish a coordinated, governmentwide agency effort to engage recipients, and share audit findings.

- ## U.S. Department of State

State is the de facto shared service provider for the Federal government's foreign affairs activity overseas. These services include hosting the USAID financial management system, and providing other shared services such as budget execution, accounts payable, general ledger accounting, cashiering, and disbursement for over 45 Federal entities. State remains very active with FIT, as well as intelligence and security agencies as further shared services are discussed. This supports efforts to lead and transform Federal financial management by reducing duplicate work at multiple agencies and devising new automated solutions. State and FIT will continue to look at ways to expand foreign affairs shared services by identifying and facilitating potential implementations of operational capabilities (e.g. consolidated invoice processing and centralized receivables management) that help reduce costs and increase transparency. State's contributions will help to provide improved solutions for the foreign affairs community, including financial and logistics management.

- **U.S. Department of Transportation**

DOT has been working to optimize Federal financial system management consistent with the vision and goals of the FM LoB. For example in FY 2013, DOT employed resources to modernize their reimbursement agreement process in the Federal financial management system to improve quality, performance and reduce cost consistent with the goals of the FM LoB. DOT is also working on upgrading their Federal financial management system, which will improve the timeliness and accuracy of data available for decision making. DOT's upgrade will also facilitate stronger internal controls and reduce costs by providing a Shared Service Provider (SSP) solution to its operating administrations and other Federal clients.

DOT also established a governance and oversight structure of its _www.USAspending.gov_ data quality initiative in FY 2013. An integrated project team is now dedicated to improving financial assistance business practices and services. The team includes executive sponsorship from all DOT Operating Administrations (OA) in financial management, systems, and procurement. DOT is working towards establishing baseline procedures of the current www.USAspending.gov reporting process to gain an understanding of current validation and reconciliation processes of each OA. DOT plans on testing baseline procedures and establishing a process to measure the accuracy of quarterly reporting in FY 2014. DOT's long term goal is to improve and standardize reporting, validation and reconciliation processes across the department.

DOT is also working with the Award Committee for E-Government and other Federal agencies on the various financial spending systems (e.g. _www.USAspending.gov_, sub-recipient reporting, Central Contractor Registry, and the Data Universal Numbering System) to enable greater transparency of Federal spending and improved agency operations. DOT's contributions will help to provide improved solutions for the financial management community, including financial assistance program management and reporting, and enhanced alignment among the financial assistance communities. This will benefit the DOT OA, SSP Federal clients, and the broader financial management community.

- **U.S. Department of Veterans Affairs**

The FM LOB enables VA to improve reporting transparency of Federal spending to stakeholders including the Congress and the public. The FM LoB improves the consistency and quality of VA data across all financial spending communities, including acquisitions and financial assistance.

- **U.S. Agency for International Development**

The FM LoB benefits USAID by enhancing timely and accurate data for decision-making, standardizing financial management-related systems, business processes, and data elements, and making reliable and international assistance financial data available to the public. FIT is working with USAID to enhance the shared service approach currently in place between USAID and the Department of State. Specifically, USAID is able to leverage improved financial management services with the Department of State, who currently serves as a Center of Excellence and hosts USAID's financial management system. USAID is also able to leverage operational capabilities (e.g., invoice processing and centralized receivables management) that FIT identifies and implements, helping to reduce costs and increase transparency.

In addition, the FM LoB allows USAID to improve public reporting of Federal spending on international assistance. Further, the ongoing effort to standardize, optimize, and consolidate agency financial systems being led as part of the FM LoB helps USAID address financial management-related system redundancy and data standardization.

- **Environmental Protection Agency**

The EPA benefits from participation in the FM LoB through the implementation of standards, requirements, and tools to support EPA's financial management functions. The EPA also benefits from cross-government information sharing on financial systems implementation best practices and standards. In FY 2013, EPA initiated its Grants Management Transformation Initiative (GMTI). The purpose of the GMTI is to explore how to achieve efficiencies in grants management, while enhancing quality and accountability. The key elements of this initiative will continue into 2014 when the agency will evaluate the cost effectiveness and feasibility of implementing GMTI recommendations for system and process improvements.

- **General Services Administration**

Through the FM LoB, GSA provided Financial Management services and financial oversight and expertise to 44 financial management clients, which includes internal customers and other agencies. Smaller agencies are able to avoid costs associated with creating their own financial management capabilities. Agencies, including GSA, also avoid costs associated with investing in IT infrastructure that support financial management, and may also receive personnel savings because employees are able to focus on their agency's missions versus provided financial management expertise. In FY 2013, GSA successfully transferred the managing partner role to Treasury. Aligning the FM LoB with other governmentwide strategic financial management functions at Treasury eliminated redundancy, and enhanced clean opinion audit reports.

- **National Aeronautics and Space Administration**

The FM LoB leads efforts to transform Federal financial management, reduce costs, increase transparency, and improve delivery of agencies' missions by operating at scale, relying on common standards, shared services, and using state-of-the-art technology. NASA benefits from the FM LoB because it provides a forum for Federal agencies to share information, and weigh pros and cons of various initiatives, in particular exploring options for improving financial systems through the use of shared services. NASA also benefits from the support provided by the FM LoB to standardize core financial business processes and data elements, provide reliable and accessible financial data to the public, provide adequate training and development resources to agency workforces ensure strong oversight of Federal programs using tools such as the Single Audit.

- **Nuclear Regulatory Commission**

NRC supports FIT's efforts to transform Federal financial management by devising new automated solutions. NRC is in the process of enhancing its financial system to approve invoices within the system as a prerequisite to participating in the Internet Payment Platform System, a web-based network for processing transactions between agencies and suppliers. In addition the NRC has deployed an integrated acquisition system that has automated each step of the acquisition and procurement processes that will receive payment information from the financial system. Together, these efforts will eliminate manual processes, enhance efficiencies in payment processing, and result in improved financial management services across the acquisitions and payments community.

- **National Science Foundation**

In FY 2013, the FM LoB began initiative planning and engagement with the partner agencies. Ultimately, NSF's contributions will help to provide improved solutions for the financial management community including financial assistance program management and reporting, and enhanced alignment among the financial assistance communities. This will benefit all funding bureaus within NSF, and the overall financial management community.

The FM LoB will also enable NSF to improve reporting transparency of Federal spending to stakeholders including the Congress and the public. The FM LoB will improve the consistency and quality of NSF data across all financial spending communities including acquisitions and financial assistance. For example, one of the FM LoB's goals, in collaboration with the COFAR, is to foster more efficient and effective Federal financial management by coordinating the development and implementation of a standardized business process, data standards, metrics, and information technology. NSF will potentially be able to utilize the FM LoB initiative to reach out to other agencies and departments that have modernized their financial system for best practices and lessons-learned as NSF transitions from its disparate, aging financial management system to a fully integrated financial management solution known as iTRAK).

Additionally, the FM LoB was recently expanded to encompass the former Grants Management Line of Business. The strategies to align the financial assistance and financial management communities around effective and efficient management of funds and priorities are still being developed, but will ultimately provide NSF many benefits going forward.

- **Office of Personnel Management**

FIT has actively engaged OPM CFO senior executives in planning efforts and defining new standards for Shared Service Providers in alignment with OMB Memorandum M-13-08. In FY 2013, OPM's CFO transitioned accounts payable functions to a Federal shared service provider. FIT has recognized OPM's continued efforts improve financial management systems by leveraging shared service solutions. OPM will benefit from being actively engaged in FIT working groups to define standards and guidance for Federal shared service providers, internal shared service providers, and private shared service providers.

FIT's effort to work with and evaluate each agency's progress in adopting a shared service approach has been very beneficial to OPM in determining the direction for the Consolidated Business Information System (CBIS), OPM's core financial system. OPM currently operates with a Federal shared service provider which performs accounts payable functions in CBIS, and a private vendor which serves as as the systems integrator for CBIS. Because of OPM's unique approach to adopting shared service, FIT has invited OPM to participate in working groups and offer lessons learned to other agencies. FIT works with OPM and other agencies to continue to improve the various financial spending systems (e.g. USASpending.gov and FPDSNG) enabling greater transparency of Federal spending and improved operations.

In addition, the FM LoB guidance and standardization has enabled taxpayer savings by reducing administrative burdens, and addressing any possibilities for waste, fraud, and abuse. OPM's contributions to the FM LoB will help fund improved solutions for the financial management community. OPM's unique approach to transitioning to shared service has also resulted in reduced costs and increased transparency. By bringing together the financial management communities, the FM LoB will enable improved agency coordination and internal operations.

- **Small Business Administration**

Treasury's assumption of responsibility for the FM LoB in FY 2013 is a significant accomplishment for governmentwide transparency efforts. Treasury's responsibility over cross-agency financial management transparency solutions will help SBA and the broader financial management community to streamline financial management and assistance business processes and data management practices.

Treasury established a program management infrastructure for the FM LoB, enabling SBA to easily participate in the initiative. Treasury conducted specific the FM LoB planning activities on behalf of all partner agencies, including establishment of MOUs with partner agencies, and coordination and engagement with key stakeholders. The FM LoB will enable SBA to improve business processes, reduce the cost of financial systems, leverage strategic sourcing opportunities, and identify and recaptures improper payments, and prevents payment errors before they occur to protect taxpayer resources from waste, fraud, and abuse.

- **Social Security Administration**

Treasury's assumption of responsibility of FM LoB in FY13 provided leverage for the Office of Financial Innovation and Transformation (FIT) to lead efforts to transform Federal financial management by reducing duplicate work at multiple agencies, devising new automated solutions, and assisting OMB in developing a long-term financial management systems strategy. This will assist SSA and the broader financial management community to streamline financial management and data management practices.

SSA's contributions to the FM LoB will contribute toward the development of common automated solutions for transaction processing, such as the Internet Payment Platform, which SSA has successfully piloted. This effort allows Federal agencies and associated suppliers to obtain transactional information relating to Federal payments. SSA's participation in this program is an example of how SSA has, and will continue to adopt the latest guiding principles for system modernization by embracing common automated solutions. Overall, the FM LoB will enable SSA to improve the consistency and quality of data across all financial spending communities including acquisition and financial management.

Geospatial Line of Business (Geo LoB)

Managing Partner: U.S. Department of the Interior

- **U.S. Department of Agriculture**

USDA fully supports the intent of deploying Geo LOB as the operational implementation of prior Federal Geographic Data Committee (FGDC) geospatial infrastructure strategy, standards, and data coordination. As a participating member of the FGDC Steering Committee, USDA endorses the recent executive leadership strategy and goals.

USDA anticipates an immediate return on investment from the Geo LOB with respect to improved use of centralized channels to distribute data and information to agricultural and natural resources management and conservation stakeholders. The formation of the new National Geospatial Platform (NGP) increases opportunities for enhanced public services. Federal, state, local, regional and tribal government as well as the general public may equitably leverage the open cloud NGP to search, collaborate, refine, and innovate with USDA data and services.

The NGP environment provides USDA with a new alternative for testing offerings, publishing USDA geospatial assets, measuring public demand, and providing a common channel to increase speed to market, which may result in internal costs savings and avoidance. USDA seeks to define and validate NGP content management performance measures so as to determine data and service demand, capacity management, and public relevancy of USDA geospatial assets. With evidence of this ranking and use behavior, USDA can better attend high value assets, align scarce resources, and increase the contribution to decision-making through enhanced views, extension to new mission requirements or customer needs, and combinations with other mission content. However, USDA anticipates greater participant value in FY 2014 as implementation issues are further defined and resolved, and new services are deployed in direct partnership with other FGDC member agencies.

- **U.S. Department of Commerce**

The Geospatial Platform activities benefit DOC by increasing efficiencies and reducing costs for services. DOC also benefits from coordination between agencies participating in the Geo LoB and services between Federal agencies, their state and local partners, and the public.

The process of identifying National Geospatial Data Assets for DOC resulted in data collections that will be valuable for DOC communities of interest. A prototype agency community was developed for the National Oceanic and Atmospheric Administration (NOAA) on the Geospatial Platform in FY 2013. DOC anticipates migrating all content from the NOAA GeoPlatform to the National Geospatial Platform in FY 2014, resulting in cost savings.

NOAA has also benefitted from its participation in the Geo LoB GeoCloud initiative. NOAA programs are very interested in the potential opportunities inherent in commodity cloud services for its geospatial activities. Lessons were learned through participation in the GeoCloud project that benefit NOAA efforts to contract for cloud services. The Geo LoB has made DOC aware of tools for managing and implementing standards such as the ISO metadata standard.

- **U.S. Department of Defense**

Within DOD, geospatially enabling traditional business data has improved business process efficiency, allowed for geographically based analytic and investment processes, improved infrastructure asset tracking, improved mission delivery, and promoted the use of business intelligence in the DOD's decision support systems. DOD is using geospatial information and analysis to improve its auditability, specifically with regard to establishing completeness of the DOD real property inventory.

The Geo LoB has the potential to benefit DOD through improved sharing of geospatial information, cost avoidance by reducing the creation of duplicative geospatial information, and collaborative planning with partner agencies for the applications of geospatial information and services to support national defense priorities. To date, DOD has only been able to contribute small amounts of data to the Federal Geospatial Platform. This is primarily due to information security and data sensitivity considerations, however DOD is committed to pursuing greater collaboration and sharing of data within the constraints of information security protocols.

At this time, DOD does not have quantifiable benefit metrics that gauge the success of the initiative in supporting national defense missions during FY 2013. However, continuing and diligent engagement between DOD and the Federal Geographic Data Committee regarding the Geospatial Platform shows great promise for significantly increasing DOD data and content contributions during FY 2014.

- **U.S. Department of Education**

ED participates in the Federal Geographic Data Committee (FGDC)'s GeoCloud II Program, which provides ED with an opportunity to explore the Amazon Web Services (AWS) hosting platform for its geospatial applications. Through the GeoCloud program, ED's National Center for Education Statistics (NCES) gained experience with cloud-based Windows 2008R2 Server and ESRI ArcGIS for Server 10.1 platform. This resulted in a successful migration of its on-premises ArcGIS platform for the School District Demographic System (SDDS). In particular, ED was able to migrate the information system supporting the SDDS Map Viewer. This is a publicly available application, which includes a mobile version, providing access to information about demographics, social characteristics, and economics of children and school districts from NCES. It is the only system in the United States to nationally visually link exact school geographic locations to their demographic and economic characteristics.

Success for NCES equates to high availability, increased efficiency, and increased innovation with a platform that supports rapid deployment of its geospatial solutions for accessing school district demographic and related geographic data. Since deployment in the Geocloud Program, NCES has added two new geospatial solutions to its architecture. NCES, with support from the U.S Census Bureau, started collecting school boundaries for over 13,000 districts, and is using the cloud servers to support this effort. As with school district files, NCES disseminates data from sources such as the U.S. Census

Bureau's American Community Survey mapped against school boundaries. For the first time, relationships between schools in the same district or across the nation can be examined.

The *Demographic Profile Viewer* is the latest innovation to be supported by the cloud services. This viewer provides policymakers, education professionals, researchers, and the public a unique way to better understand patterns in our school systems. It visually presents key demographic data within school districts and school boundaries nationwide, measuring approximately 600 economic and social characteristics from the ACS profile data and 2010 Decennial Census.

- **U.S. Department of Energy**

The Geo LoB allows DOE to collaborate more closely with Federal and state partners to share ideas and support cross cutting solutions such as the Geospatial Platform, Data.Gov and other geospatial related initiatives, to reduce cost to the government and improve services across DOE and to citizens. The collaboration realized through the Geo LoB enables DOE to share ideas and showcase the geospatial services DOE provides. DOE submitted candidate systems for consideration for both the Geospatial Platform and the National Geospatial Value Proposition from the Office of Energy Efficiency and Renewable Energy, Knowledge Discovery Framework, U.S. Energy Information Administration, and the Interactive Energy Disruption Map. DOE also submitted a candidate system for the GeoCloud called the Homeland-Defense Operational Planning System from our Lawrence Livermore National Laboratory. DOE has also contributed 211 datasets thru the public facing Data.Gov interface that includes geospatial data. Visualizations of spatially-referenced energy data can be found on *www.data.gov/energy/page/energy-maps*. These maps provide insight into regional, industrial, and economic factors that influence energy consumption and generation across the United States. DOE submissions support the Geo LoB initiative, and highlight DOE's commitment to coordinate efforts with Federal, state and private partners to reduce costs, improve the quality of services DOE provides, and increase efficiency across DOE.

DOE has benefited from the information exchange between agencies participating in the Geospatial LoB. The sharing of DOE data through the Geospatial Platform and Data.Gov results in improved service benefits to citizens, and Federal and state partners by reducing cost for data. DOE received benefits from our participation in the Geo LoB by effectively and efficiently sharing geospatial capabilities and ideas in a shared geospatial environment. DOE's relationships with partners developed through the Geo LoB would not have been realized otherwise.

- **U.S. Department of Health and Human Services**

HHS benefits from the Geo LoB adoption of additional information exchange standards, facilitating improved sharing of Geospatial data, applications, and services between Federal government agencies, state and local partners, and the public. The Geo LoB's efforts to revise the National Geospatial Infrastructure Strategic Plan will help HHS plan how to best utilize the improved geospatial information services.

- ## U.S. Department of Homeland Security

The DHS Geospatial Management Office (GMO) is the designated steward and portfolio manager responsible for advancing the Geospatial Program objectives by planning for, acquiring, configuring, and implementing Homeland Security Enterprise geospatial information and technology shared services and off-the-shelf products for use across DHS missions. The Geospatial working group provides DHS-wide program governance through oversight, management directives, and an executive steering committee which helps DHS prioritize need, and revise the way DHS acquires and pays for geospatial enterprise systems and services. Executive steering committee membership has expanded to include representatives from 23 DHS offices. The governance process has contributed to operational efficiencies across DHS operations centers and geospatial programs, while ensuring DHS-wide investment requests are strategically and fiscally aligned.

In addition, the DHS GMO, with the support from the DHS Office of the Chief Procurement Officer, is facilitating the procurement of new enterprise-wide geospatial technical support services, geospatial data and geospatial software contracts to consolidate existing geospatial investments, or close capability gaps. The GMO also renewed enterprise software contracts for geospatial software and coordinated with FGDC and NGA on reuse of the Homeland Security Infrastructure Protection data product and other national geospatial data assets. Implementing DHS-wide contract vehicles and procurements enable consolidation and elimination of redundant contract management efforts and systems while also closing capability gaps. This achieves cost-savings, and also provides DHS components with easier access to geospatial software and support services.

- ## U.S. Department of Housing and Urban Development

HUD utilizes the Geo LoB to enable easier access to, and sharing of, relevant spatial data sets and capabilities across the government. HUD receives a return on investments from the Geo LoB with regards to greater efficiency and synergy within the HUD and across the Federal government. Geospatial data and information are critical components for meeting HUD's mission to create strong, sustainable, inclusive communities and quality, affordable housing.

The Geo LoB improves productivity, mission delivery, and services to citizens. The Geo LoB also enables HUD's traditional business data to improve business process efficiency, allowing for place-based planning and execution of its mission objectives. The Geo LoB improved HUD's business processes by enabling easier access to and sharing of relevant spatial data sets and capabilities across government. HUD is also able to leverage the Geo LoB's broad purchasing power to stand up shared infrastructure and services, such as the Geospatial Platform, at a fraction of the cost it would take to implement comparable capabilities independently.

- ## U.S. Department of Justice

DOJ continues to benefit from the information exchange between agencies participating in the Geo LoB, which promotes increased sharing of Geospatial data, applications, and services between Federal Government agencies, their state and local partners, and the public. The LoB focus on improving the _www.GeoPlatform.gov_ collaboration and information sharing site has increased the data assets available for use by DOJ and its components and partner organizations. The efforts of the Geo LoB in identifying the core A-16 National Geospatial data assets will lead to improved services as more data sets,

APIs, and data sharing tools are published to the National Geospatial Platform and the maturity and quality of these assets is documented as part of the A-16 portfolio management process.

- **U.S. Department of State**

State benefits from the information exchange between agencies participating in the Geo LoB, which promotes increased sharing of Geospatial data, applications, and services between Federal Government agencies, their state and local partners, and the public. The Geo LoB's focus on identifying the core National Geospatial data assets is leading to improved services as the datasets are published on the National Geospatial Platform.

- **U.S. Department of Transportation**

DOT benefits from the sharing of geospatial data and information amongst the agencies participating in the Geo LoB. The Geo LoB's focus on identifying the core National Geospatial data assets will lead to more reliable and readily available geospatial information, particularly as these assets are published to the Geospatial Platform. DOT anticipates future benefits as DOT develops community and agency pages on the Geospatial Platform.

- **U.S. Department of the Treasury**

Compared to other Federal agencies, Treasury is not a big consumer of geospatial data. The only agency within Treasury with any Geospatial information is the Office of the Comptroller of the Currency. Even within that office, very little geospatial data and software is utilized. However, Treasury supports the work being performed by the Geo LoB partners to develop standards, applications, data sets and services for use by Federal entities, state, local and tribal partners. Treasury and other partner agencies have worked collaboratively to develop standards and products that have resulted in a more coordinated approach to producing, maintaining, and using geospatial data. This work will improve services for all entities that use the assets developed by the Geo LoB.

- **U.S. Department of Veterans Affairs**

VA has benefited from the information exchange between agencies participating in the Geo LoB which promotes increased sharing of Geospatial data, applications, and services between Federal Government agencies, their state and local partners, and the public. VA's contribution to the Geo LoB, will allow the Department to leverage the Federal Government's broad purchasing power to stand up shared infrastructure and services, at a fraction of the cost it would take to implement comparable capabilities independently.

- **U.S. Agency of International Development**

USAID benefits from the information exchange between agencies participating in the Geo LoB, which promotes increased sharing of Geospatial data, applications, and services between Federal agencies, their state and local partners, and the public. The Geo LoB's focus on identifying core National Geospatial data assets will lead to improved services as the data sets are published to the National Geospatial Platform, and their maturity and quality clearly documented as part of the portfolio management process.

- ## U.S. Army Corps of Engineers

The Geo LoB has the potential to benefit USACE through improved sharing of Geospatial data information, cost avoidance by reducing the creation of duplicative geospatial information, and collaborative planning with partner agencies for the applications of geospatial information to support the USACE mission. USACE anticipates that the Federal Geoplatform will enable government-to-citizen and citizen-to-government geospatial information sharing that USACE would otherwise be unable to undertake.

- ## Environmental Protection Agency

The EPA continues to benefit from the extensive information exchange between agencies participating in the Geo LoB. This work has increased EPA staff knowledge of data resources available to support the EPA's missions, and led to EPA participation in standards development that will enhance data consistency and thus value of these critical data assets. EPA benefits from National Geospatial Datasets that are registered, tagged, and published them on the National Geospatial Platform. The availability of these datasets improves the ability for EPA users to search, discover, and access to data used in mission business processes. Enhanced access to critical data and associated analytical capabilities will improve EPA's ability to plan, target, and implement its work as well as create environmental indicators. The value these datasets will provide to EPA will continue to increase as additional datasets are published.

In addition, in FY 2013 EPA's Office of Water and Office of Environmental Information was able to begin to evaluate the use of the National Geospatial Platform hosting environment for national water data services and applications. More quantitative benefits are anticipated in FY 2014 when some of these services are put into production. Finally, in FY 2013, there was an agreement to formally affiliate the Homeland Infrastructure Field Level Database (HIFLD) Working Group with the Geo LoB FGDC Subcommittee. This will facilitate consistent data management across the two organizations, increase the use of authoritative versions of data for homeland security and emergency responses, and reduce development redundancies by making the HIFLD Freedom data available through the Geospatial Platform. Once in place this will increase the efficiencies of homeland security and emergency response efforts at EPA.

- ## General Services Administration

The Geo LoB supports a coordinated approach to producing, maintaining, and using geospatial data within the Federal government. This approach allows GSA to review and leverage existing geospatial data created by partner agencies, rather than initiating redundant and costly business-driven geospatial analysis within the agency.

GSA has actively participated in geospatial data collection efforts and helped to establish a baseline for benchmarking and measuring geospatial costs and anticipated efficiencies. By providing a point of contact for the Inventory of Owned and Leased Properties, GSA has increased the request for data from other agencies and improved our communication between agencies. In addition, GSA is the lead agency for the Real Property Data Theme. A working group was established by GSA to craft a Real Property Asset Data Content Standard. The purpose of this standard is to create a basic standard for which all future real property standards can be based to improve data quality and standards for this theme. The rough draft was completed and submitted to the Federal Geographic Data Committee's review process in FY 2013.

- **National Aeronautics and Space Administration**

NASA benefits from the information exchange between agencies participating in the Geo LoB, which promotes increased sharing of Geospatial data, applications, and services between Federal agencies, their state and local partners, and the public. The Geospatial LoB's focus on identifying core National Geospatial data assets will lead to improved services as the data sets are published to the National Geospatial Platform, and their maturity and quality clearly documented as part of the portfolio management process.

- **National Archives and Records Administration**

NARA benefits from the information exchange between agencies participating in the Geo LoB, which promotes increased sharing of Geospatial data, applications, and services between Federal agencies, their state and local partners, and the public. The Geospatial LoB's focus on identifying core National Geospatial data assets will lead to improved services as the data sets are published to the National Geospatial Platform, and their maturity and quality clearly documented as part of the portfolio management process.

- **National Science Foundation**

NSF benefits from the information exchange between agencies participating in the Geo LoB, which promotes increased sharing of Geospatial data, applications, and services between Federal agencies, their state and local partners, and the public. The Geo LoB's focus on identifying core National Geospatial data assets will lead to improved services as the data sets are published to the National Geospatial Platform, and their maturity and quality clearly documented as part of the portfolio management process.

- **Small Business Administration**

SBA benefits from the information exchange between agencies participating in the Geospatial LoB, which promotes increased sharing of Geospatial data, applications, and services between Federal agencies, their state and local partners, and the public. The Geo LoB's focus on identifying core National Geospatial data assets will lead to improved services as the data sets are published to the National Geospatial Platform, and their maturity and quality clearly documented as part of the portfolio management process.

- **Social Security Administration**

SSA is a very modest consumer of geospatial technology, and is just learning how to take advantage of data sharing opportunities that may be available through the Geospatial platform. During FY2013, the inter-agency Geospatial Platform came to life, and will become a valuable tool for supporting collaboration and open data strategies using map visualizations to better communicate with government, industry and citizens. The Geo LoB is focused on developing an inter-agency shared service environment. SSA is undergoing technical alignment with the Geo LoB Platform, and has not yet been able to exploit data sharing through the platform. However, SSA looks forward to utilizing the platform during FY 2014. In addition, SSA benefits from the information exchange between agencies participating in the Geo LoB, which promotes increased sharing of Geospatial data, applications, and services between Federal agencies, their state, local, and tribal partners, and the public.

Human Resources Line of Business (HR LoB)

Managing Partner: Office of Personnel Management

- ### U.S. Department of Agriculture

USDA developed One USDA, an enterprise-wide, modern, cost-effective, standardized, and interoperable HR solution that aligns with the HR LoB. One USDA provides common core functionality to support the strategic management of HR, and improve mission delivery through the deployment of an integrated workforce system. One USDA also facilitates strategic and advisory HR service delivery and streamlined HR transaction execution, providing managers with uniform HR policies across USDA, improving data integrity, and providing the capability to utilize a staffing report based on budgeted, approved positions.

Prior to the development of One USDA, each of USDA's 29 agencies and staff offices used separate HR systems to perform more than 90% of the same functions. In most cases, data had to be entered numerous times. One USDA promotes one-time data entry, saving HR professionals' time, and allowing them to focus on more strategic human capital priorities such as recruitment, and improving the on-boarding process of new hires. In addition to saving time, USDA has realized over $1.0 million in cost-savings by using one staffing solution across all agencies.

In addition, in FY 2013, USDA selected the eRecruit/Entry-on-DutyOnline (EODOnline) staffing solution to be utilized across the entire department. This system will provide a variety of benefits, including standardized vacancy announcement formatting, interview process design, a standardized on-boarding process, and one-time data entry. USDA worked collaboratively with all agencies to define requirements, design and test the system. USDA has recently conducted fice User Acceptance Testing of the eRecruit/EOD Online system and achieved end-to-end integration.

- ### U.S. Department of Commerce

DOC implemented a phased migration to the technology solution of an HR LOB Shared Service Center (SSC) beginning in FY 2012. The HR LOB SSC migration has substantially improved the effectiveness, efficiency and quality of human capital services provided by DOC, and delivered a substantial return on investment in both cost-savings and cost-avoidance. For example, DOC's seven HR service centers (excluding the Census Decennial) manually processed approximately 210,000 personnel actions in FY 2013. The processing of these actions via an automated system has resulted in a reduction in personnel time, postage fees, and error rates. Conservative estimates show that by automating this process, DOC will save approximately 42,000 labor hours, at an estimated value of $3.50 million.

To date, DOC has migrated 71% of all DOC employees to HR Connect, an OPM certified HR LoB Shared Services Provider, and plans to migrate the remaining balance when DOC migrates NOAA and International Trade Administration field employees in FY 2014. When DOC migrated 14,527 U.S. Census Bureau's non-decennial employees to Treasury's HR Connect, 56% of all managers successfully authenticated within the first week. 511 unique routing rules help to direct HR actions from managers to specific HR Subject Matter Experts (SMEs), which helps expedite and streamline HR processes, significantly improving the processing of HR actions. HR Connect eliminates inefficiencies of manual transaction processing, duplicate data entry and manual reporting processes. It also allows for custom built award limits, which help monitor and enforce policy guidelines for managers processing awards for employees.

In addition, migration to the technology solution of an HR LoB SSC provides significant tangible benefits to DOC, including cost-savings and avoidance from HR management activities through automated core personnel processes and decommissioning multiple cuff systems. DOC also benefits from operational efficiencies and improved customer service by delivering self-service functionality and access to HR data and transactions to managers and employees. Human capital strategic planning, decision making and workforce analytics are also enhanced though self-service access to enterprise-wide HR data by DOC executives, managers and human capital personnel.

Finally, DOC completed several strategic assessment sessions with the Census Decennial HR operations teams, Treasury's HR Connect Program Office, and other industry experts and vendor partners for the purpose of identifying a roadmap of next steps to help contribute to the reduction of the overall spend generated by the Census Decennial activities to provide the following additional benefits. These assessments identified opportunities for Census Bureau cost reductions. This future partnership with Treasury could provide automated and standardized HR process and workflows that eliminate redundant transaction processing, set the stage for DOC to realize significant operational cost-savings and cost-avoidance, and provided federal agencies with an updated and robust payroll service provider built on newer, non-mainframe technology.

- **U.S. Department of Defense**
DOD provides core civilian personnel operations, accounting, and financial functions for its Military Services, Defense Agencies and civilian customer agencies through the Defense Civilian Personnel Advisory Service (DCPAS) and the Defense Finance and Accounting Service (DFAS). These initiatives allow the DOD to optimize the cost of managing HR and payroll systems and processes across a worldwide customer base, reducing costs incurred by performing these functions individually.

As the DOD enterprise civilian HR system manager, DCPAS successfully migrated the Navy's Defense Civilian Personnel Data System (DCPDS) regional HR systems, and other unique systems, to the Denver Data Center which supports DCPDS enterprise operations. The relocation was completed four (4) days ahead of schedule with all systems on line on August 30, 2013, operating effectively without any technical issues. Maximizing the use of virtualization and cloud computing is also in progress. These enhancements complement the consolidation of DCPDS operations to a single site, and provide customers (e.g., HR professionals, supervisors, managers, and employees) simplified user access and improved problem resolution time. In addition, information assurance is improved through software and hardware enhancements, as well as configuration control and system management within a consolidated environment, all while reducing costs incurred due to reductions in energy consumption, space/facility requirements, and reduced operational labor costs.

In addition, DFAS completed the first two phases of a 3-phase implementation of the Enterprise Human Resources Integration-Retirement Data (EHRI-RD), and expects to complete its final and last phase in FY 2014. The EHRI-RD standardizes and automates the retirement data collection. It aims to modernize the retirement system, upgrade a mission-critical legacy system that supports the retirement process, and migrate from a paper-based environment to an electronic system of retirement data management. EHRI-RD will allow employees to get their full annuity payments in a timelier manner, and reduces the amount of time it takes to get OPM retirement information for employees who have recently retired or deceased. With the completion of this project, DFAS will be in a position to begin testing with the OPM sometime next year.

- **U.S. Department of Education**

ED's Human Capital and Client Services benefits from the HR LOB by utilizing the HR LOB SSC model to achieve maximum cost savings and leverage shared federal requirements in obtaining and implementing commercial off-the-shelf products. ED's SSC partner, the DOI Interior Business Center (IBC), automates HR functions, and can be used with commercial off-the-shelf products to provide talent recruitment and management, workforce management, and time and attendance. The portfolio of products provides real-time (or near real time) integration with the Federal Personnel and Payroll System, thus reducing duplicate data entry and reducing effort needed to create and manage multiple user accounts. In addition, implementation of time keeping solutions like Krono's WebTA eliminated the use of paper timecards, paper leave approvals, and manual timekeeper time and attendance, thus providing transparent time and attendance management, and electronic audit records. Web-based employee input also provides self-verification of time and leave, reducing entry error and increasing accuracy. ED will continue to explore other offerings by IBC to gain cost-savings through economies of scale, automate processes, and eliminate duplicate and manual data entry and to contribute and learn from other federal agency best practices through the SSC consortium.

- **U.S. Department of Energy**

As a result of a feasibility study, DOE is in the process of assessing the DOI IBC SSC. DOE is determining IBC's ability to meet functional and technical requirements as well as identifying detailed costs for the services and products they provide. This in-depth analysis is intended to reveal how well DOE fits into IBC's shared service delivery model, the gaps that have to be addressed, and provide detailed comparisons showing IBC costs as compared to the costs of existing DOE HR IT infrastructure. The desired outcome is to build a robust business case analysis that will aid senior leadership in making an informed decision on DOE's path forward for HR and payroll delivery. In addition, DOE is a partnering member of the Multi-Agency Executive Strategy Committee (MAESC), and has been able to network and leverage other agency migration initiatives.

- **U.S. Department of Health and Human Services**

HHS is one of the approved HR LoB service providers, and provides a comprehensive portfolio of HR services and systems to 12 HHS customer agencies with approximately 80,000 employees. Following the development of a comprehensive business case in FY 2012 and OPM approval in FY 2013, the HHS Service and Supply Fund approved funding to migrate the Core HR, payroll, time and attendance, and reporting functions to the USDA's shared HR environment at their National Finance Center (NFC). The NFC solution is an HR LoB-approved solution which contains four components directly associated with current HHS HR IT support functionality. The NFC solution will support current HHS HR strategic and operational requirements through a fully integrated approach.

Outsourcing to NFC will provide HHS with a tightly integrated reporting capability without additional HHS investments for future enhancement. HHS also formed a program office dedicated to the coordination and joint delivery of the NFC solutions. The program office is responsible for managing the coordination of HHS migration to the new platform. The program office focuses on governance, functional transition, business transformation, and operations transition. A master program schedule is in place, and day-to-day coordination of activities is in progress. HHS is establishing benefits metrics and will monitor NFC performance during both implementation and operational periods.

HHS expects to realize significant cost-savings from this initiative, including savings from HR IT systems, HR staffing, and savings achieved by reducing the number of contracts for similar services. HHS also anticipates operational efficiencies including improved employee productivity attributed to the implementation of an automated personnel action process.

- **U.S. Department of Homeland Security**
The HR IT Program resides within the DHS Office of the Chief Human Capital Office. The goal of the program is to consolidate, integrate, and modernize core HR systems across DHS components by reducing redundancy and increasing functionality and efficiency in support of new business requirements to allow executives to focus on mission-critical issues.

Human Capital Business Systems (HCBS) is the designated steward and portfolio manager responsible for advancing the program mission by planning for, acquiring, and implementing HR LoB shared services, and other HR systems and services to consolidate, modernize, and/or replace HR IT systems and address capability gaps at the Department-level.

While DHS currently operates four enterprise solutions: NFC Corporate (Payroll/Personnel), Empow-HR (Personnel), webTA (Time and Attendance), and the eOPF (Electronic Personnel Folders), significant opportunities exist within the HR LOB for additional cost savings and service improvements. Enterprise-wide contract vehicles and procurements enable consolidation and elimination of redundant contract management efforts and systems while also closing capability gaps identified during the Human Capital Segment Architecture study completed in 2011.

For example, in May 2013, DHS awarded a blanket purchase agreement (BPA) for an Enterprise Talent Management System (ETMS) to consolidate nine Learning Management Systems into one, and provide an integrated employee performance management system. This Software as a Service application is hosted in the vendor's public cloud under the Federal Risk and Authorization Management Program (FedRAMP) certified infrastructure. When fully deployed, managers will have the ability to link employee performance goals with organizational goals while also being able to connect employees with career-development training opportunities.

In addition, in September 2013 DHS awarded a BPA for medical workers compensation case management services. This service delivery provides employees with early intervention and case management by a medical professional who also acts as an employee advocate. Components also have immediate access to claims, case files, data, and reports to support claims management. Data and reporting enhances Components ability to detect fraud, prevent organizational hazards, and improve processes. By pursuing these services, Components can significantly reduce waste and misuse of workers compensation benefit payments to employees and medical providers, reduce payments for substitute or temporary employees who fill in for injured employees, and save time, thereby enabling HR professionals to focus on their other HR duties.

- **U.S. Department of Housing and Urban Development**

The shared services delivery model within the HR LoB Initiative enables HUD to standardize all major HR business functions and processes and the systems that support them, and achieve significant savings. Since the implementation of HUD's HR LoB-certified SSC core transaction processing system, HUD has achieved over $10.70 million dollars in cost-avoidance. Also, HUD is utilizing the HR End-to-End project, a solution which provides an automated one-stop-shop for human capital management services from the beginning of the HR lifecycle when an employee is acquired, until the end when an employee leaves the department. This solution improves tracking and reporting capabilities, leads to improved customer satisfaction, better workflow management, faster and more accurate service delivery, and cost savings achieved through integrating disparate systems and automating manual process.

The HR LoB shared service delivery model also supports improved management, operational efficiencies, and improved customer service. HUD's participation in the MAESC and the Customer Council has provided an opportunity to contribute to the goals and objectives of the HR LoB and provide a forum for knowledge sharing, and networking across the various agencies. In FY 2013, HUD continued initiative planning and engagement with OPM and other HR LoB partner agencies through participation in the MAESC, and worked to provide improved solutions for two of the most critical functions, staff acquisition and performance management.

Specifically, in FY 2013, and improved recruitment and staffing functionality was deployed, which has improved HUD's capacity to recruit talent within OPM's 80-day hiring criteria, and improved the quality of job analysis and assessment questions created. Position classification functionality was also deployed to a pilot group, which will improve the quality of employees' position descriptions and alignment with actual job duties and responsibilities. Additionally, performance assessment functionality was released in FY 2013 which, for the first time, enabled HUD to:

- Create cascading Specific, Measurable, Assignable, Realistic, and Time-Related (SMART) goals;

- Automatically populate the annual review with mid-year review ratings and comments;

- Ensure all employees have equal time for each step in the performance management (PM) process;

- Provide system generated e-mail messages for each step in the PM process; and,

- Established a 360-degree peer review.

- **U.S. Department of the Interior**

The DOI IBC was selected as one of four federal e-Payroll providers and one of six federal HR SSCs in 2004. The IBC offerings include both core and non-core HR systems as defined by OPM. In the area of core systems, IBC provides personnel and payroll processing for all DOI bureaus and offices as well as 42 other non-DOI clients using the Federal Personnel and Payroll System (FPPS). FPPS is a fully integrated personnel and payroll processing application and database. It allows for real-time updates and edits of employee's personnel and payroll data, and enhances timeliness and accuracy of agency pay actions, reduces paperwork, standardizes and automates essential administrative services and processing, and improves financial performance. IBC also offers several options for time and attendance (T&A) reporting. Each T&A system allows clients to include project or cost accounting data with the time entries, and the systems interface readily with FPPS for streamlined service.

Results of FPPS User Group meetings, email surveys, and performance metrics indicate that the needs of FPPS owners and users are being met. For example, in July 2013, IBC earned an overall customer service excellence rating of 8.34 out of 10 based on customer satisfaction surveys. In FY 2013, the HR Directorate met all of the performance metrics defined in the service level agreement. For example, FFPS was available to customers 99.96% of the time, and payroll staff was available 100% of the time. In addition, the Configuration Change Board (CCB) provides assurance that client needs, all related legislative changes, and upgrades are incorporated into the FPPS releases.

In the area of non-core systems, IBC offers the HR Management Suite (HRMS). HRMS includes an integration framework that enables real-time interoperability between FPPS and other systems, a talent management system (TMS) that consists of SuccessFactors' learning management and performance management modules, a workforce transformation and tracking system (WTTS), an entry on duty system (EODS), and OPM's Electronic Official Personnel File (eOPF) system. WTTS and EODS are integrated real-time with FPPS and with the Talent Acquisition Systems. The Talent Acquisitions Systems include Monster Government Solution's Enterprise Hiring Manager and OPM's USA Staffing.

As IBC expands its customer base, DOI's costs remain steady, although it is clear that managing HR services is more than simply reducing or maintaining costs. DOI has identified several challenges that affect the ability to perform its mission including critical skills shortages, retirement losses, difficulty retaining promising young employees, dependence on seasonal or volunteer workforces, and insufficient diversity in the workforce, to name a few. This investment has assisted DOI in meeting the challenges through common solutions, such as standard position descriptions and vacancy announcements, streamlined hiring processes, workforce planning, and competency-based human capital management.

- **U.S. Department of Justice**

DOJ supports the HR LoB by participating in modernization, integration, and performance assessment initiatives. In return, DOJ leverages governmentwide HR IT consolidation initiatives and standardized reference models. For example, DOJ has completed its migration of Payroll Administration and Benefits Administration to shared services delivered by the National Finance Center - two core functions provided under the HR LoB. DOJ is also assessing Federal SSC capabilities for a planned migration for Personnel Action Processing delivery.

One component of DOJ, the Bureau of Alcohol, Tobacco, Firearms and Explosives (ATF), already utilizes the Personnel Action Processing SSC, which was transferred to DOJ when ATF realigned from Treasury to DOJ in 2003. ATF's shared service provider enables "paperless" mechanisms, such as personnel action and performance management workflow, allowing ATF to achieve efficiencies in human resources-related processes. For example, ATF has a workforce of approximately 5,000 employees. In FY 2013, ATF completed 3,030 employee performance work plans using an automated performance management workflow system. ATF expects to complete another 1,000 performance work plans that were delayed due to the government shutdown by the end of December 2013. ATF's shared service provider's automated system also provides a mechanism to notify managers when employees are due a within grade pay increase (WGI). Managers are electronically notified and are asked to respond electronically to certify employees are performing at an acceptable level and are eligible for a WGI. This automated method gives the HR office advanced notice to withhold a WGI if necessary. Similarly, managers are notified of employees' anniversary date for potential career ladder promotions. Managers are given sufficient time to initiate an action and ensure employees receive their promotions on-time. DOJ expects that other components within the department will achieve similar benefits as the department continues toward migrating to an SSC for Personnel Action Processing.

Additionally, all DOJ components have either implemented, or are in the process of implementing, the eOPF service provided by OPM. This capability will allow all employees to access their electronic OPF. DOJ's eOPF program provides department-wide policy and guidance to components on eOPF issues, configuration changes/updates, and resolves DOJ-wide user issues. All employees currently receive, or will receive, e-mail notifications within 24 hours when there are updates to their eOPF.

Finally, DOJ has also transitioned to the Web Time and Attendance (WebTA) product offered through the National Finance Center and implemented the system allowing employees to record their own time electronically. This replaced the department's manual system of recording time, has greatly enhanced the control environment associated with time and attendance administration, and has drastically reduced the number of payroll errors. WebTA allows for the entry of leave and premium pay requests, the validation and certification of time entered, and the capture of Time Utilization and Record Keeping data, which is used to track time for Special Agents, Investigative Analysts and other identified groups such as Investigative Classification so that it can be mapped to the program/subprogram as needed.

- **U.S. Department of Labor**

DOL began its migration to an HR LoB Core HR Transactional System SSC in FY 2011. The migration is projected to accomplish a substantial return on investment through cost savings and cost avoidance delivered by the HR LOB model of sharing infrastructure and eliminating duplicative systems. The migration will also upgrade DOL's software platform, providing significant operational and technological benefits. By moving to a modern technology platform, DOL will benefit from improved vendor support, easier integration, and increased security. Through implementation of new functionality and additional automation, DOL can reduce the workload on its HR staff, improve data quality, and provide better service to its employees. In FY 2013, DOL completed all applicable business and funding agreements with the Department of the Treasury HR SSC. Completion of these funding documents provides funding limits and establishes cost control mechanisms. The documents also define change management processes and the procedures both parties will use to limit new scope and increases in cost. These agreements will enable the project to progress and provide necessary governance structure. DOL and Treasury mutually benefit from having a solid governance base required for project implementation. The agreements clearly outline the responsibilities of both parties for a successful migration.

DOL and Treasury also completed the functional design and development of DOL customizations, in addition to cleansing all critical data issues during mock conversions. System walkthroughs and focused testing was accomplished with the help of over 150 subject matter experts from across DOL and Treasury, and user acceptance, integration, and pilot testing will be completed by the beginning of FY 2014. By conducting in-depth functional design, and involving stakeholders from across DOL agencies, regions, and functional, operational, and technical areas, all key constituents were informed and actively engaged throughout process. DOL increased stakeholder support for the project, acquired critical commitments to participate throughout the migration project, and was able to fully understand the changes that will occur as a result of the HR LoB implementation. This hands-on participation will help streamline system and business process adoption throughout DOL.

Although DOL invested a significant amount of staff time and effort to support functional design, data cleanup, and testing, DOL will be able to recoup the costs associated with implementation by FY 2017. DOL estimates $3,880,668 in cost-savings by using Treasury's SSC solution compared to DOL's current HR solution. DOL also estimates $97,817,924 in cost-avoidance by calculating costs which would have been incurred to enhance DOL's current HR solution to match the functional and technical capabilities of Treasury SSCs solution.

- **U.S. Department of State**

The Integrated Personnel Management System provides superior human capital management in support of State's diplomatic mission. It directly addresses goals in the Quadrennial Diplomacy and Development Review, in particular, the high priority performance goal of HR Management of Building Civilian Capacity. The Executive Office of the Bureau of Human Resources is the designated steward and portfolio manager responsible for advancing the IPMS program mission by planning for, acquiring, configuring, and implementing HR LoB shared services, and off-the-shelf packages for use across the enterprise.

In addition, State participated in the HR LoB benchmarking study, which tracks the progress made toward achieving its vision and goals. HR benchmarking provides insight into successful practices at other agencies and private enterprises. The insight that participating agencies can take away from this study is a significant benefit, particularly given the continuing expectation that agencies do more with fewer resources. In particular, it is important for State to be able to identify trends over time, including HR cost per employee serviced, and the HR servicing ratio. State may use these trends to analyze expenditures which reflect overall budget fluctuations, and other organizational conditions, such as hiring surges, hiring freezes, and sequestration. State can also determine where they are positioned in relation to the Federal aggregate, and identify the components that comprise the majority of HR spending. Further research into these components may provide insight into whether the HR budget is optimally allocated, and in turn, allow State to identify efficiencies.

- **U.S. Department of Transportation**

DOT's participation in the MAESC and the Customer Council provides an opportunity to directly influence the future of the services encompassed by the HR LoB. In addition, DOT migrated to the DOI IBC under the payroll consolidation initiative, and is aligning DOT HR IT with the vision and goals of the HR LoB and the SSC concept.

For example, in January 2013 DOT completed the implementation of the Workforce Transformation Tracking System WTTS pre-employment module, which allows HR personnel to send required forms necessary for completion during the pre-employment process. This enables DOT to streamline the onboarding process. DOT was also the first IBC partner to go live with the implementation of the system interface between WTTS, EODS and TMS. This allows new hires that have been cleared through the security process to complete their necessary DOT training via the internet prior to their day-one orientation. In FY 2014, IBC will be implementing the separation module for employees leaving DOT. This will ensure faster processing of the separating employee and ensure all DOT assets are accounted for prior to the employee's last day.

Additionally, DOT's is one of the first IBC partners to pilot the Monster Government Solutions (MGS) Position Description Library. Monster Position Classification helps automate and sustain HR hiring standards during a time of decreased staffing, and can significantly reduce the time required to create and maintain position descriptions. The MGS system provides continuity, consistency and accuracy of classifications across DOT. Positions can be more easily standardized and grade levels across DOT are more easily evaluated.

The HR LoB provides services to DOT employees at a reduced cost, enabling resources that were historically devoted to developing and maintaining HR systems to become available for other purposes. Through the use of the automated systems and processes, DOT expects to achieve even greater efficiencies at reduced costs. DOT's ability to be part of the design and decision-making process for HR automation in the Federal government also helps ensure DOT's needs are considered in the development of future services.

- **U.S. Department of the Treasury**

As one of the six public sector designated SSCs, Treasury strives to provide continuously improved functionality which directly supports the strategic vision of its customers while driving down the individual costs of these functions. The HR LoB includes successful partnerships between Treasury's HR Connect (which delivers human capital systems) and Fiscal Service Administrative Resource Center (which provides individual customer servicing offices and a full suite of HR operational and transactional service) and the USDA's National Finance Center (which provides payroll processing and support). The HR LoB has successfully provided these partnered services to the Federal government for over 10 years. Presently, Treasury HR LoB services are utilized by more than 30 Federal organizations, and will service over 210,000 employees by FY 2015.

Through its partnerships, Treasury's services cover HR strategy, organization and position management, staff acquisition, performance management, compensation management, benefits management, HR development, employee and labor relations, EODS, and separation management. Treasury offers customers an employee and manager decision-based portal that is single sign-on with the HR system, and Enterprise Data Management Workforce Analytics capabilities. Treasury continues to modify core products as well as introduce new non-core products to further enhance capabilities and satisfy customer needs.

In FY 2013, Treasury, in partnership with DOC, transitioned seven DOC components to Treasury's online solution. Additionally, Treasury completed preparations for transitioning DOL. Agencies realize benefits by being able to focus on improved management, operational efficiencies, cost savings and/or avoidance, and improved customer service. These benefits allow agencies to transform their internal HR focus from an emphasis on administrative processing to strategy planning support for the agency leadership and increased customer service and counseling for managers and employees.

Treasury is focused on providing human capital services supporting the entire lifecycle and has accomplished a number of initiatives in the non-core systems such as solutions supporting Integrated Talent Management (ITM). Specifically in FY 2013, Treasury configured and implemented a new ITM system for four customers (HUD, USAID, SBA, and various offices/bureaus within Treasury). Treasury collaborated with its customers and its partners to configure and implement performance management, dashboard reporting, competency assessments, learning management, development plans and social networking through the use of communities. In collaboration with its customers, the Treasury configured and deployed the system on a global level, allowing current customers and the future customer-base to leverage a globally-deployed secure system. One major benefit of the expansion of non-core services to customers includes the proven scalability of these Treasury HR LoB components to allow for additional methodology and global opportunities. This also allows for common processes and systems for Federal employees. Treasury also completed the first phase of the implementation of operational HR servicing for HUD's Office of Housing, to include staff acquisition, position classification, employee benefits, personnel action processing, personnel security, HR systems help desk support, and HR reporting.

- **U.S. Department of Veterans Affairs**
Migrating to the HR LoB SSC will replace VA's legacy HR system and provide significant upgrades in VA's ability to process personnel actions as well as capture and report HR information. The new HR information system will eliminate manual transactions and paper driven processes by allowing VA employees and HR managers to access a common system for all HR transactions. The new system will provide all core HR functionality, and will interface with other VA financial and HR systems, including the Defense Finance and Accounting Service e-payroll solution, VA's electronic Official Personnel Folder, and VA's time and attendance solution.

The overall goal is to improve efficiency and effectiveness of HR processes by acquiring a state-of-the-art, 21st century solution from an approved HR SSC provider. VA strives for improvements in effectiveness and productivity by leveraging IT to streamline HR processes that support and track the veteran population. By acquiring an HR solution that supports the core HR functions, VA will be able to improve its HR processing and ensure that it is able to support the HR community, customers, employees, and veterans. Using state-of-the-art technology, will also enable the VA to improve recruitment, hiring, and retention efforts, and invest in workforce development in a way that supports fulfillment of the VA's commitment to veterans and their families.

The VA anticipates achieving cost-savings by migrating to a SSC and replacing its current legacy system. Savings are expected to be achieved by avoiding costs for services that would otherwise be contracted out, such as EODS and HR tracking solutions.

- **U.S. Agency for International Development**

In FY 2013, USAID implemented a new ITM system provided by Treasury. USAID collaborated with Treasury to configure and implement performance management, dashboard reporting, competency assessments, learning management, development plans and social networking through the use of communities.

USAID also transitioned to Treasury's online HR solution, avoiding costs that would have been incurred for USAID to implement or upgrade duplicative systems. USAID benefits from this transition by being able to focus on improved management, operational efficiencies, cost savings and/or avoidance, and improved customer service. These benefits allow USAID to transform their internal HR focus from an emphasis on administrative processing to strategy planning support for the agency leadership and increased customer service and counseling for managers and employees.

- **Environmental Protection Agency**

EPA benefits from HR LoB through its use of compensation management services and systems provided by one of the approved payroll providers, the DOD's Defense Finance Accounting Service. EPA's planned future involvement in HR LoB is to migrate additional HR systems to an approved HR service provider. In so doing, EPA will achieve the benefits of "best-in-class" HR solutions and will be able to offer managers and employees across the agency improved services without the cost of developing and maintaining its own HR system. EPA's involvement in the HR LoB benefits the agency through a community of practice that is dedicated to the efficient and effective implementation of HR solutions, the development of best practices and lessons learned, and governmentwide strategic HR management.

Additionally, EPA has benefitted from the use of an HR LoB talent acquisition system. The upgraded system enables electronic document exchange, which benefits job applicants, HR office personnel, and selecting officials by providing automatic updates and reducing manual processes. Vacancy processing times have improved based on the electronic document acceptance and the removal of physical mail wait time.

- **General Services Administration**

The HR LoB allows GSA to realize economies of scale through a shared service provider concept. Shared service providers offer state-of-the-art, timely, and cost-effective HR services. GSA contributions to the HR LoB initiative help shape a governmentwide solution, and identify best practices and lessons learned that benefit all government agencies. In an effort to optimize cost savings, GSA is reviewing options for the delivery of HR IT services, and has issued a request for information to Federal HR LoB providers to further review options, and ensure maximum efficiency in the delivery of HR services.

In FY 2013, GSA participated in the planning of an HR shared service strategy, enabling GSA stakeholders to focus on HR missions that are aligned with HR IT solutions, and realize efficiencies in staff time and costs. GSA also participated in an HR LoB customer forum for potential customers, which allowed potential customers to assess HR LoB provider options while enabling GSA to minimize their travel and marketing costs.

- **National Aeronautics and Space Administration**

NASA's Human Capital programs tightly align with the HR LoB to create governmentwide, cost-effective, interoperable HR tools in support of the strategic management of human capital. NASA leverages a strong collaborative relationship with the DOI IBC, which enables NASA to access IBC systems and tools. NASA developed a plan that automates the feed between the FPPS, NASA's on-boarding tool, and the WTTS, and will integrate a secure file transfer to eOPF. The integration provides NASA with the ability to quickly and accurately on-board new employees, and ensures timely and secure access to appropriate IT resources while reducing manual data entry requirements. NASA's WTTS system enhances system functionality to leverage data across multiple systems, and will generate cost-savings in the coming years. Focus on efficiency and effectiveness of shared service providers also enables NASA to gain information about the degree to which the providers are demonstrating results against a set of business practices.

The HR LoB also implemented an assessment program for approved HR LoB providers. The HR LOB conducted assessments of HR LoB service providers, including the DOI IBC which NASA utilizes as a shared service provider. Provider improvements as a result of assessments strengthen the personnel payroll system. Assessments also provide a communication mechanism to ensure a strong agency role in funding and other decisions that affect NASA.

- **National Science Foundation**

NSF utilizes the DOI IBC as a personnel and payroll provider. The ability to acquire the HR solutions and services from an SSC reduces the burden and simplifies the processes for managing multiple systems and services. This approach allows NSF to pursue its core grants management mission rather than developing and managing legacy HR applications.

For example, in FY 2013, NSF continued its integration of web-based time and attendance (WebTA) into NSF's HR operations. NSF provided strong support for the establishment of a WebTA user group and participated actively in the first user group meeting. NSF planned to acquire services offered by the IBC contract rather than contracting directly with a service provider, which will allow NSF to realize significant savings on an annual basis. Finally, NSF began investigating the potential use of other IBC shared HR services, including the WTTS and EODS systems.

Through DOI IBC services, NSF has been able to reduce resources from the business of developing and maintaining legacy, core HR systems. Resources historically devoted to maintaining an outdated, custom time and attendance system are available for other NSF mission-critical functions.

Recreation One-Stop

Managing Partner: U.S. Department of Agriculture

- **U.S. Department of the Interior**

DOI realized numerous benefits by participating in *www.Recreation.gov* in FY 2013. The website contains trip planning resources, and is an advanced reservation service for over 3,000 Federal recreation facilities. In FY 2013, visitors made over 1.40 million reservations for DOI recreation areas generating over $14.0 million in revenue for the agencies. *Recreation.gov* is also working collaboratively with DOI Travel and Tourism officials to market DOI's public lands to both domestic and international visitors. Marketing efforts are included in the contract and come at no additional cost to DOI.

- **U.S. Army Corps of Engineers**

USACE is continuously expanding offerings on *www.Recreation.gov* to enhance recreation information and reservation opportunities. In FY 2013, USACE helped facilitate the re-design of the *www.Recreation.gov* home page, and enhanced the recreation information database (RIDB) to include new photos, activity and destination information, and itineraries. The new information includes all Federal lands available for recreation, not just for activities and parks requiring reservations. Adding additional inventory improves access to facilities, reservations, and Federal recreation information and opportunities. Additionally, an improved homepage design will attract more visitors to *www.Recreation.gov*. It also improves marketing, and provides additional public lands information to a variety of stakeholders. For example, the featured places and articles change about once a month, providing many opportunities to showcase USACE places, events, and recreation opportunities. The enhanced RIDB can also be leveraged by different stakeholders, including the recreation community, service providers, and chambers of commerce, to encourage travel and itinerary planning.

USACE was able to modify an existing contract to provide additional web design services at a lower cost. Increased public utilization of the site will help offset the redesign costs. Finally, enhancing this service and the information in the inventory will continue to minimize duplication and redundancy associated with multiple reservation systems.

APPENDIX B: SOURCES OF FY 2014 E-GOVERNMENT INITIATIVE AND LINES OF BUSINESS FUNDING BY DEPARTMENT/AGENCY AND BUREAU

In accordance with section 732(b)(3) of the Act, this table shows the distribution of FY 2014 department/agency contributions by E-Government initiative and line of business as reported by agencies. Agency contributions reflect commitments of funding and/or in-kind services provided by partner agencies to initiative managing partner agencies in support of the initiative or line of business. Contribution amounts are determined annually through collaborative, inter-agency E-Gov initiative governance structures and are subject to approval by OMB. "In-kind contributions" represent the dollar equivalent of contribution of services made by an agency in support of the initiative. Such contributions represent non-cash funding, and may include the contribution of equipment, facilities, software, license fees, and/or FTEs.

Given that the Act only requires the report to include E-Government initiatives sponsored by OMB, initiatives, this report does not include initiatives funding by "fee-for-service" contributions. "Fee-for-service" contributions represent transfers of funds by partner agencies to initiative service providers in exchange for services rendered by initiative service providers. The amounts are typically based on a transaction/usage-based fee structure (e.g., for payroll processing, payroll service providers base their service fees on the number of employees at a customer agency). Initiative service providers use fees collected from partner agencies to cover ongoing operational costs, perform routine maintenance, and support their customer base.

Agency contributions reflect commitments of funding and/or in-kind services provided by partner agencies to initiative managing partner agencies in support of the initiative or line of business. Contribution amounts are determined annually through collaborative, inter-agency E-Gov initiative governance structures and subject to approval by OMB. In-kind contributions represent the dollar equivalent of contribution of services made by an agency in support of the initiative. Such contributions represent non-cash funding, and may include the contribution of equipment, facilities, software, license fees, FTEs, etc.

This report does not include initiatives funding by "fee-for-service" contributions. "Fee-for-service" contributions represent transfers of funds by partner agencies to initiative service providers in exchange for services rendered by initiative service providers. The amounts are typically based on a transaction/usage-based fee structure (e.g., for payroll processing, payroll service providers base their service fees on the number of employees at a customer agency). Initiative service providers use fees collected from partner agencies to cover ongoing operational costs, perform routine maintenance, and support their customer base.

APPENDIX B
SOURCES OF FY 2014 E-GOVERNMENT INITIATIVE AND LINES OF BUSINESS FUNDING BY DEPARTMENT/AGENCY AND BUREAU (INCLUDES IN-KIND CONTRIBUTIONS)

Bureau	Budget Formulation and Execution LoB	Disaster Assist Improvement Plan	Financial Management LoB	Geospatial LoB	Human Resources Management LoB	Recreation One-Stop	Bureau Total
Agricultural Marketing Service	$2,663		$4,696		$7,313		$14,672
Agricultural Research Service	$7,435		$13,111		$20,418		$40,964
Animal and Plant Health Inspection Service	$7,353		$12,965		$20,191		$40,509
Departmental Administration	$482		$850		$1,324		$2,656
Economic Research Service	$362		$639		$995		$1,996
Executive Operations	$231	$180	$409		$638		$1,458
Farm Service Agency	$11,874	$55,655	$20,937		$32,606		$121,072
Food and Nutrition Service	$1,283	$6,012	$2,262		$3,522		$13,079
Food Safety and Inspection Service	$9,053		$15,963		$24,860		$49,876
Foreign Agricultural Service	$987		$1,741		$2,711		$5,439
Forest Service	$31,739		$55,964		$87,154	$200,000	$374,857
Grain Inspection, Packers and Stockyards Administration	$671		$1,183		$1,842		$3,696
National Agricultural Statistics Service	$1,135		$2,002		$3,118		$6,255
National Appeals Division							$0
National Institute of Food and Agriculture	$385		$678		$1,056		$2,119
Natural Resources Conservation Service	$10,445	$48,956	$18,417		$28,681		$106,499
Office of Chief Economist							$0
Office of Civil Rights	$126		$222		$345		$693
Office of Communications	$81		$142		$222		$445
Office of the Chief Financial Officer	$1,307		$2,305		$3,589		$7,201
Office of the Chief Information Officer	$1,043		$1,838	$225,000	$2,861		$230,742
Office of the Executive Secretariat	$22		$38		$59		$119
Office of the General Counsel	$292		$515		$801		$1,608
Office of the Inspector General	$541		$955		$1,487		$2,983
Office of the Secretary							$0

APPENDIX B
SOURCES OF FY 2014 E-GOVERNMENT INITIATIVE AND LINES OF BUSINESS FUNDING BY DEPARTMENT/AGENCY AND BUREAU
(INCLUDES IN-KIND CONTRIBUTIONS)

Bureau	Budget Formulation and Execution LoB	Disaster Assist Improvement Plan	Financial Management LoB	Geospatial LoB	Human Resources Management LoB	Recreation One-Stop	Bureau Total
Risk Management Agency	$474	$2,222	$833		$1,302		$4,831
Rural Business Cooperative Service							$0
Rural Development	$5,016	$23,513	$8,845		$13,775		$51,149
Rural Housing Service							$0
Rural Utilities Service							$0
Department of Agriculture Total	**$95,000**	**$136,538**	**$167,510**	**$225,000**	**$260,870**	**$200,000**	**$1,084,918**

APPENDIX B
SOURCES OF FY 2014 E-GOVERNMENT INITIATIVE AND LINES OF BUSINESS FUNDING BY DEPARTMENT/AGENCY AND BUREAU
(INCLUDES IN-KIND CONTRIBUTIONS)

Department of Commerce

Bureau	Budget Formulation and Execution LoB	Disaster Assist Improvement Plan	Financial Management LoB	Geospatial LoB	Human Resources Management LoB	Bureau Total
Bureau of Industry and Security	$1,016	$112	$927		$1,436	$3,491
Bureau of the Census	$10,104	$1,110	$9,220		$32,296	$52,730
Departmental Management	$748	$82	$683		$3,416	$4,929
Economic and Statistical Analysis	$1,153	$127	$1,052	$112,500	$1,896	$116,728
Economic Development Administration	$5,350	$588	$4,882		$849	$11,669
International Trade Administration	$5,068	$557	$4,625		$8,939	$19,189
Minority Business Development Agency	$311	$34	$284		$395	$1,024
National Institute of Standards and Technology	$8,766	$963	$7,999		$10,402	$28,130
National Oceanic and Atmospheric Administration	$52,511	$5,770	$47,920	$112,500	$43,897	$262,598
National Technical Information Service	$188	$21	$171		$687	$1,067
National Telecommunications and Information Administration	$1,121	$123	$1,023		$1,013	$3,280
Office of Inspector General	$270	$30	$247		$481	$1,028
US Patent and Trademark Office	$18,394	$2,021	$16,786		$24,728	$61,929
Department of Commerce Total	**$105,000**	**$11,538**	**$95,819**	**$225,000**	**$130,435**	**$567,792**

APPENDIX B
SOURCES OF FY 2014 E-GOVERNMENT INITIATIVE AND LINES OF BUSINESS FUNDING BY DEPARTMENT/AGENCY AND BUREAU
(INCLUDES IN-KIND CONTRIBUTIONS)

Department of Defense						
Bureau	Budget Formulation and Execution LoB	Federal Health Architecture LoB	Financial Management LoB	Geospatial LoB	Human Resources Management LoB	Bureau Total
Department-wide	$105,000	$2,656,000	$187,342	$42,000	$260,870	$3,251,212
Department of Defense Total	**$105,000**	**$2,656,000**	**$187,342**	**$42,000**	**$260,870**	**$3,251,212**

APPENDIX B
SOURCES OF FY 2014 E-GOVERNMENT INITIATIVE AND LINES OF BUSINESS FUNDING BY DEPARTMENT/AGENCY AND BUREAU
(INCLUDES IN-KIND CONTRIBUTIONS)

Department of Education						
Bureau	Budget Formulation and Execution LoB	Disaster Assist Improvement Plan	Financial Management LoB	Geospatial LoB	Human Resources Management LoB	Bureau Total
Departmental Management	$105,000		$230,616	$25,000	$65,217	$425,833
Office of Federal Student Aid		$35,577				$35,577
Department of Education Total	**$105,000**	**$35,577**	**$230,616**	**$25,000**	**$65,217**	**$461,410**

APPENDIX B
SOURCES OF FY 2014 E-GOVERNMENT INITIATIVE AND LINES OF BUSINESS FUNDING BY DEPARTMENT/AGENCY AND BUREAU (INCLUDES IN-KIND CONTRIBUTIONS)

Department of Energy					
Bureau	**Budget Formulation and Execution LoB**	**Financial Management LoB**	**Geospatial LoB**	**Human Resources Management LoB**	**Bureau Total**
Departmental Administration	$105,000	$124,236	$50,000	$65,217	$344,453
Department of Energy Total	**$105,000**	**$124,236**	**$50,000**	**$65,217**	**$344,453**

APPENDIX B
SOURCES OF FY 2014 E-GOVERNMENT INITIATIVE AND LINES OF BUSINESS FUNDING BY DEPARTMENT/AGENCY AND BUREAU
(INCLUDES IN-KIND CONTRIBUTIONS)

Department of Health and Human Services

Bureau	Budget Formulation and Execution LoB	Disaster Assist Improvement Plan	Federal Health Architecture LoB	Financial Management LoB	Geospatial LoB	Human Resources Management LoB	Bureau Total
Administration for Children and Families	$4,421	$37,980		$9,720		$2,558	$54,679
Administration on Aging	$4,421	$1,356		$9,720		$207	$15,704
Agency for Healthcare Research and Quality	$4,421		$60,011	$9,720		$566	$74,718
Centers for Disease Control and Prevention	$13,263	$9,495	$535,100	$29,161	$48,255	$19,246	$654,520
Centers for Medicare and Medicaid Services	$13,263	$6,728	$535,100	$29,161		$9,232	$593,484
Departmental Management	$7,738	$1,356	$1,221,570	$16,770	$1,028	$4,059	$1,252,521
Food and Drug Administration	$13,263		$535,100	$29,161		$23,054	$600,578
Health Resources and Services Administration	$13,263	$13,564		$29,161	$717	$3,258	$59,963
Indian Health Services	$13,263	$12,208	$100,019	$29,161		$29,783	$184,434
National Institutes of Health	$13,263	$33,910	$535,100	$29,161		$34,284	$645,718
Office of the Inspector General						$3,188	$3,188
Substance Abuse and Mental Health Services Administration	$4,421	$6,782		$9,720		$1,000	$21,923
Department of Health and Human Services Total	**$105,000**	**$123,379**	**$3,522,000**	**$230,616**	**$50,000**	**$130,435**	**$4,161,430**

APPENDIX B
SOURCES OF FY 2014 E-GOVERNMENT INITIATIVE AND LINES OF BUSINESS FUNDING BY DEPARTMENT/AGENCY AND BUREAU (INCLUDES IN-KIND CONTRIBUTIONS)

Bureau	Budget Formulation and Execution LoB	Disaster Assist Improvement Plan	Disaster Management Program	Financial Management LoB	Geospatial LoB	Human Resources Management LoB	Information Systems Security LoB
Domestic Nuclear Detection Office	$577			$979	$1,236	$151	
Federal Emergency Management Agency	$23,847	$17,990,000	$5,229,053	$40,458	$51,101	$11,708	
Federal Law Enforcement Training Center	$454			$771	$974	$1,284	
Federal Protective Service	$2,289			$3,884	$4,906	$1,489	
Management	$1,011		$35,503	$1,715	$2,166	$1,595	
National Protection and Program Directorate	$2,140			$3,631	$4,586	$1,756	
National Protection and Program Directorate - U.S. Visit							
Office of Health Affairs	$293			$497	$627	$118	
Office of the Inspector General	$253			$429	$542	$795	$2,590,000
Office of the Secretary of Management	$217			$368	$465	$775	
Operations Coordination and Intel & Analysis	$566		$568,969	$961	$1,213	$988	
Science & Technology Directorate	$1,462		$177,519	$2,481	$3,134	$572	
Transportation Security Administration	$13,444		$960,420	$22,809	$28,809	$66,582	
U.S. Citizenship & Immigration Services	$5,285		$462,458	$8,967	$11,326	$12,458	
U.S. Coast Guard	$17,528		$1,636,810	$29,738	$37,560	$9,567	
U.S. Customs & Border Protection	$21,068		$924,916	$35,743	$45,146	$71,206	
U.S. Immigration & Customs Enforcement	$9,926		$924,916	$16,840	$21,270	$23,594	
U.S. Secret Service	$3,255		$249,436	$5,522	$6,975	$8,221	
Working Capital Fund	$1,385			$2,347	$2,964	$667	
Department of Homeland Security Total	**$105,000**	**$17,990,000**	**$11,170,000**	**$178,140**	**$225,000**	**$213,526**	**$2,590,000**

APPENDIX B
SOURCES OF FY 2014 E-GOVERNMENT INITIATIVE AND LINES OF BUSINESS FUNDING BY DEPARTMENT/AGENCY AND BUREAU (INCLUDES IN-KIND CONTRIBUTIONS)

Department of Housing and Urban Development

Bureau	Budget Formulation and Execution LoB	Disaster Assist Improvement Plan	Financial Management LoB	Geospatial LoB	Human Resources Management LoB	Bureau Total
Management and Administration	$105,000	$132,692	$230,616	$50,000	$65,217	$583,525
Department of Housing and Urban Development Total	**$105,000**	**$132,692**	**$230,616**	**$50,000**	**$65,217**	**$583,525**

APPENDIX B
SOURCES OF FY 2014 E-GOVERNMENT INITIATIVE AND LINES OF BUSINESS FUNDING BY DEPARTMENT/AGENCY AND BUREAU
(INCLUDES IN-KIND CONTRIBUTIONS)

Bureau	Budget Formulation and Execution LoB	Disaster Assist Improvement Plan	Financial Management LoB	Geospatial LoB	Human Resources Management LoB	Recreation One-Stop	Bureau Total
Bureau of Indian Affairs and Bureau of Indian Education	$12,234	$5,938	$14,475		$15,197		$47,844
Bureau of Land Management	$15,605	$7,574	$18,463		$19,385	$50,000	$111,027
Bureau of Ocean Energy Management	$861	$418	$1,019		$1,070		$3,368
Bureau of Reclamation	$8,112	$3,937	$9,598		$10,077	$50,000	$81,724
Bureau of Safety and Environmental Enforcement	$1,153	$560	$1,364		$1,433		$4,510
Insular Affairs	$62	$30	$73		$77		$242
National Indian Gaming Commission	$185	$90	$219		$230		$724
National Park Service	$32,654	$15,850	$38,635		$40,564	$50,000	$177,703
Natural Resources Damage Assessment and Restoration	$13	$3	$17		$18		$51
Office of Inspector General	$402	$195	$476		$499		$1,572
Office of Surface Mining Reclamation and Enforcement	$795	$386	$941		$987		$3,109
Office of the Secretary	$2,252	$1,093	$2,665		$2,798		$8,808
Office of the Solicitor	$662	$322	$784		$823		$2,591
Office of the Special Trustee for American Indians	$980	$476	$1,160		$1,217		$3,833
United States Fish and Wildlife Service	$13,986	$6,788	$16,548		$17,374	$50,000	$104,696
United States Geological Survey	$12,815	$6,220	$15,163	$800,000	$15,919		$850,117
Wildland Fire Management	$41	$20	$48		$50		$159
Working Capital Fund/ Franchise	$2,188	$1,062	$2,588		$2,717		$8,555
Department of the Interior Total	**$105,000**	**$50,962**	**$124,236**	**$800,000**	**$130,435**	**$200,000**	**$1,410,633**

APPENDIX B
SOURCES OF FY 2014 E-GOVERNMENT INITIATIVE AND LINES OF BUSINESS FUNDING BY DEPARTMENT/AGENCY AND BUREAU
(INCLUDES IN-KIND CONTRIBUTIONS)

Department of Justice

Bureau	Budget Formulation and Execution LoB	Disaster Assist Improvement Plan	Financial Management LoB	Geospatial LoB	Human Resources Management LoB	Bureau Total
Bureau of Alcohol, Tobacco, Firearms, and Explosives		$2,690	$5,421	$3,529	$10,938	$22,578
Department-wide		$1,148	$396		$1,819	$3,363
Drug Enforcement Administration		$4,719	$9,529	$6,429	$18,905	$39,582
Federal Bureau of Investigation		$19,635	$37,816	$25,025	$83,507	$165,983
Federal Prison System		$18,841	$38,487		$88,328	$145,656
General Administration	$105,000		$208			$105,208
Interagency Law Enforcement			$140			$140
Legal Activities and US Marshals		$14,230	$21,968	$12,652	$55,028	$103,878
National Security Division		$193	$409		$717	$1,319
Office of Justice Programs		$1,970	$9,802	$2,365	$1,456	$15,593
United States Parole Commission		$36	$60		$172	$268
Department of Justice Total	**$105,000**	**$63,462**	**$124,236**	**$50,000**	**$260,870**	**$603,568**

APPENDIX B
SOURCES OF FY 2014 E-GOVERNMENT INITIATIVE AND LINES OF BUSINESS FUNDING BY DEPARTMENT/AGENCY AND BUREAU
(INCLUDES IN-KIND CONTRIBUTIONS)

Bureau	Budget Formulation and Execution LoB	Disaster Assist Improvement Plan	Financial Management LoB	Human Resources Management LoB	Bureau Total
Departmental Management	$105,000	$104,808		$65,217	$275,025
Employment and Training Administration			$141,399		$141,399
Department of Labor Total	**$105,000**	**$104,808**	**$141,399**	**$65,217**	**$416,424**

APPENDIX B
SOURCES OF FY 2014 E-GOVERNMENT INITIATIVE AND LINES OF BUSINESS FUNDING BY DEPARTMENT/AGENCY AND BUREAU
(INCLUDES IN-KIND CONTRIBUTIONS)

	Department of State					
Bureau	Budget Formulation and Execution LoB	Disaster Assist Improvement Plan	Financial Management LoB	Geospatial LoB	Human Resources Management LoB	Bureau Total
Department-wide	$105,000	$11,538	$95,892	$50,000	$65,217	$327,647
Department of State Total	**$105,000**	**$11,538**	**$95,892**	**$50,000**	**$65,217**	**$327,647**

APPENDIX B
SOURCES OF FY 2014 E-GOVERNMENT INITIATIVE AND LINES OF BUSINESS FUNDING BY DEPARTMENT/AGENCY AND BUREAU (INCLUDES IN-KIND CONTRIBUTIONS)

Bureau	Budget Formulation and Execution LoB	Financial Management LoB	Geospatial LoB	Human Resources Management LoB	Bureau Total
Department of Transportation					
Federal Aviation Administration	$21,988	$93,158	$42,358	$109,484	$266,988
Federal Highway Administration	$63,691	$87,036	$3,026	$6,650	$160,403
Federal Motor Carrier Safety Administration	$834	$6,252		$2,340	$9,426
Federal Railroad Administration	$1,736	$2,988	$813	$1,881	$7,418
Federal Transit Administration	$14,195	$19,563		$1,304	$35,062
Maritime Administration	$478	$3,022		$1,679	$5,179
National Highway Traffic Safety Administration	$1,303	$3,648	$1,090	$1,359	$7,400
Office of Inspector General	$103	$1,104		$978	$2,185
Office of the Secretary	$358	$5,736		$1,708	$7,802
Pipeline and Hazardous Materials Safety Administration	$238	$1,813	$1,797	$839	$4,687
Research and Innovative Technology Administration	$12	$5,823	$916	$1,577	$8,328
Saint Lawrence Seaway Development Corporation	$27	$24		$318	$369
Surface Transportation Board	$37	$449		$318	$804
Department of Transportation Total	**$105,000**	**$230,616**	**$50,000**	**$130,435**	**$516,051**

APPENDIX B
SOURCES OF FY 2014 E-GOVERNMENT INITIATIVE AND LINES OF BUSINESS FUNDING BY DEPARTMENT/AGENCY AND BUREAU
(INCLUDES IN-KIND CONTRIBUTIONS)

Department of the Treasury							
Bureau	Budget Formulation and Execution LoB	Disaster Assist Improvement Plan	Financial Management LoB	Geospatial LoB	Human Resources Management LoB	IRS Free File	Bureau Total
Bureau of the Public Debt			$95,892				$95,892
Internal Revenue Service						$1,555,590	$1,555,590
Working Capital Fund	$105,000	$113,462		$25,000	$260,870		$504,332
Department of the Treasury Total	**$105,000**	**$113,462**	**$95,892**	**$25,000**	**$260,870**	**$1,555,590**	**$2,155,814**

APPENDIX B
SOURCES OF FY 2014 E-GOVERNMENT INITIATIVE AND LINES OF BUSINESS FUNDING BY DEPARTMENT/AGENCY AND BUREAU (INCLUDES IN-KIND CONTRIBUTIONS)

Department of Veterans Affairs

Bureau	Budget Formulation and Execution LoB	Disaster Assist Improvement Plan	Federal Health Architecture LoB	Financial Management LoB	Geospatial LoB	Human Resources Management LoB	Bureau Total
Departmental Administration	$105,000	$67,308	$2,094,000	$158,998	$25,000	$260,870	$2,711,176
Department of Veterans Affairs Total	**$105,000**	**$67,308**	**$2,094,000**	**$158,998**	**$25,000**	**$260,870**	**$2,711,176**

APPENDIX B
SOURCES OF FY 2014 E-GOVERNMENT INITIATIVE AND LINES OF BUSINESS FUNDING BY DEPARTMENT/AGENCY AND BUREAU (INCLUDES IN-KIND CONTRIBUTIONS)

U.S. Agency for International Development

Bureau	Budget Formulation and Execution LoB	Financial Management LoB	Geospatial LoB	Human Resources Management LoB	Bureau Total
Agency-wide	$105,000	$95,819	$25,000	$65,217	$291,036
U.S. Agency for International Development Total	$105,000	$95,819	$25,000	$65,217	$291,036

APPENDIX B
SOURCES OF FY 2014 E-GOVERNMENT INITIATIVE AND LINES OF BUSINESS FUNDING BY DEPARTMENT/AGENCY AND BUREAU (INCLUDES IN-KIND CONTRIBUTIONS)

U.S. Army Corps of Engineers				
Bureau	Budget Formulation and Execution LoB	Geospatial LoB	Recreation One-Stop	Bureau Total
Agency-wide	$80,000	$50,000	$200,000	$330,000
U.S. Army Corps of Engineers Total	$80,000	$50,000	$200,000	$330,000

APPENDIX B
SOURCES OF FY 2014 E-GOVERNMENT INITIATIVE AND LINES OF BUSINESS FUNDING BY DEPARTMENT/AGENCY AND BUREAU
(INCLUDES IN-KIND CONTRIBUTIONS)

Broadcasting Board of Governors		
Bureau	**Budget Formulation and Execution LoB**	**Bureau Total**
Agency-wide	$50,000	$50,000
Broadcasting Board of Governors Total	**$50,000**	**$50,000**

APPENDIX B
SOURCES OF FY 2014 E-GOVERNMENT INITIATIVE AND LINES OF BUSINESS FUNDING BY DEPARTMENT/AGENCY AND BUREAU
(INCLUDES IN-KIND CONTRIBUTIONS)

Central Intelligence Agency		
Bureau	Human Resources Management LoB	Bureau Total
Agency-wide	$65,217	$65,217
Central Intelligence Agency Total	**$65,217**	**$65,217**

APPENDIX B
SOURCES OF FY 2014 E-GOVERNMENT INITIATIVE AND LINES OF BUSINESS FUNDING BY DEPARTMENT/AGENCY AND BUREAU
(INCLUDES IN-KIND CONTRIBUTIONS)

Environmental Protection Agency					
Bureau	Budget Formulation and Execution LoB	Financial Management LoB	Geospatial LoB	Human Resources Management LoB	Bureau Total
Agency-wide	$75,000	$95,819	$225,000	$65,217	$461,036
Environmental Protection Agency Total	**$75,000**	**$95,819**	**$225,000**	**$65,217**	**$461,036**

APPENDIX B
SOURCES OF FY 2014 E-GOVERNMENT INITIATIVE AND LINES OF BUSINESS FUNDING BY DEPARTMENT/AGENCY AND BUREAU
(INCLUDES IN-KIND CONTRIBUTIONS)

Equal Employment Opportunity Commission

Bureau	Budget Formulation and Execution LoB	Bureau Total
Agency-wide	$50,000	$50,000
Equal Employment Opportunity Commission Total	**$50,000**	**$50,000**

APPENDIX B
SOURCES OF FY 2014 E-GOVERNMENT INITIATIVE AND LINES OF BUSINESS FUNDING BY DEPARTMENT/AGENCY AND BUREAU
(INCLUDES IN-KIND CONTRIBUTIONS)

General Services Administration

Bureau	Budget Formulation and Execution LoB	Federal Asset Sales	Financial Management LoB	Geospatial LoB	Human Resources Management LoB	Bureau Total
General Activities	$105,000		$41,332		$65,217	$211,549
Real Property Activities				$50,000		$50,000
Supply and Technology Activities		$765,000				$765,000
General Services Administration Total	**$105,000**	**$765,000**	**$41,332**	**$50,000**	**$65,217**	**$1,026,549**

APPENDIX B
SOURCES OF FY 2014 E-GOVERNMENT INITIATIVE AND LINES OF BUSINESS FUNDING BY DEPARTMENT/AGENCY AND BUREAU
(INCLUDES IN-KIND CONTRIBUTIONS)

Millennium Challenge Corporation		
Bureau	**Budget Formulation and Execution LoB**	**Bureau Total**
Agency-wide	$50,000	$50,000
Millennium Challenge Corporation Total	**$50,000**	**$50,000**

APPENDIX B
SOURCES OF FY 2014 E-GOVERNMENT INITIATIVE AND LINES OF BUSINESS FUNDING BY DEPARTMENT/AGENCY AND BUREAU (INCLUDES IN-KIND CONTRIBUTIONS)

National Aeronautics and Space Administration					
Bureau	Budget Formulation and Execution LoB	Financial Management LoB	Geospatial LoB	Human Resources Management LoB	Bureau Total
Agency-wide	$105,000	$124,236	$225,000	$65,217	$519,453
National Aeronautics and Space Administration Total	$105,000	$124,236	$225,000	$65,217	$519,453

APPENDIX B
SOURCES OF FY 2014 E-GOVERNMENT INITIATIVE AND LINES OF BUSINESS FUNDING BY DEPARTMENT/AGENCY AND BUREAU
(INCLUDES IN-KIND CONTRIBUTIONS)

National Archives and Records Administration

Bureau	Geospatial LoB	Bureau Total
Agency-wide	$15,000	$15,000
National Archives and Records Administration Total	$15,000	$15,000

APPENDIX B
SOURCES OF FY 2014 E-GOVERNMENT INITIATIVE AND LINES OF BUSINESS FUNDING BY DEPARTMENT/AGENCY AND BUREAU
(INCLUDES IN-KIND CONTRIBUTIONS)

Nuclear Regulatory Commission

Bureau	Financial Management LoB	Bureau Total
Agency-wide	$41,322	$41,322
Nuclear Regulatory Commission Total	**$41,322**	**$41,322**

APPENDIX B
SOURCES OF FY 2014 E-GOVERNMENT INITIATIVE AND LINES OF BUSINESS FUNDING BY DEPARTMENT/AGENCY AND BUREAU (INCLUDES IN-KIND CONTRIBUTIONS)

National Science Foundation

Bureau	Budget Formulation and Execution LoB	Financial Management LoB	Geospatial LoB	Human Resources Management LoB	Bureau Total
Agency-wide	$105,000	$139,094	$25,000	$65,217	$334,311
National Science Foundation Total	**$105,000**	**$139,094**	**$25,000**	**$65,217**	**$334,311**

APPENDIX B
SOURCES OF FY 2014 E-GOVERNMENT INITIATIVE AND LINES OF BUSINESS FUNDING BY DEPARTMENT/AGENCY AND BUREAU (INCLUDES IN-KIND CONTRIBUTIONS)

Office of National Drug Control Policy

Bureau	Budget Formulation and Execution LoB	Bureau Total
Agency-wide	$50,000	$50,000
Office of National Drug Control Policy Total	**$50,000**	**$50,000**

APPENDIX B
SOURCES OF FY 2014 E-GOVERNMENT INITIATIVE AND LINES OF BUSINESS FUNDING BY DEPARTMENT/AGENCY AND BUREAU
(INCLUDES IN-KIND CONTRIBUTIONS)

Office of Personnel Management					
Bureau	Budget Formulation and Execution LoB	Disaster Assist Improvement Plan	Financial Management LoB	Human Resources Management LoB	Bureau Total
Agency-wide	$105,000	$41,346	$41,332	$65,217	$252,895
Office of Personnel Management Total	**$105,000**	**$41,346**	**$41,332**	**$65,217**	**$252,895**

APPENDIX B
SOURCES OF FY 2014 E-GOVERNMENT INITIATIVE AND LINES OF BUSINESS FUNDING BY DEPARTMENT/AGENCY AND BUREAU
(INCLUDES IN-KIND CONTRIBUTIONS)

Office of National Drug Control Policy

Bureau	Budget Formulation and Execution LoB	Bureau Total
Agency-wide	$50,000	$50,000
Office of National Drug Control Policy Total	**$50,000**	**$50,000**

APPENDIX B
SOURCES OF FY 2014 E-GOVERNMENT INITIATIVE AND LINES OF BUSINESS FUNDING BY DEPARTMENT/AGENCY AND BUREAU
(INCLUDES IN-KIND CONTRIBUTIONS)

Securities and Exchange Commission

Bureau	Budget Formulation and Execution LoB	Bureau Total
Agency-wide	$50,000	$50,000
Securities and Exchange Commission Total	**$50,000**	**$50,000**

APPENDIX B
SOURCES OF FY 2014 E-GOVERNMENT INITIATIVE AND LINES OF BUSINESS FUNDING BY DEPARTMENT/AGENCY AND BUREAU
(INCLUDES IN-KIND CONTRIBUTIONS)

Small Business Administration					
Bureau	Budget Formulation and Execution LoB	Disaster Assist Improvement Plan	Financial Management LoB	Geospatial LoB	Bureau Total
Agency-wide	$50,000	$70,192	$67,475	$25,000	$212,667
Small Business Administration Total	**$50,000**	**$70,192**	**$67,475**	**$25,000**	**$212,667**

APPENDIX B
SOURCES OF FY 2014 E-GOVERNMENT INITIATIVE AND LINES OF BUSINESS FUNDING BY DEPARTMENT/AGENCY AND BUREAU
(INCLUDES IN-KIND CONTRIBUTIONS)

Social Security Administration					
Bureau	Disaster Assist Improvement Plan	Federal Health Architecture LoB	Financial Management LoB	Geospatial LoB	Bureau Total
Agency-wide	$39,423	$100,000	$67,475	$25,000	$231,898
Social Security Administration Total	**$39,423**	**$100,000**	**$67,475**	**$25,000**	**$231,898**

APPENDIX C: FY 2014 FUNDING BY E-GOVERNMENT INITIATIVE AND LINES OF BUSINESS

In accordance with section 732(b)(3) of the Act, this table shows the distribution of FY 2014 department/agency contributions by E-Government initiative and line of business as reported by agencies. Agency contributions reflect commitments of funding and/or in-kind services provided by partner agencies to initiative managing partner agencies in support of the initiative or line of business. Contribution amounts are determined annually through collaborative, inter-agency E-Gov initiative governance structures and are subject to approval by OMB. "In-kind contributions" represent the dollar equivalent of contribution of services made by an agency in support of the initiative. Such contributions represent non-cash funding, and may include the contribution of equipment, facilities, software, license fees, and/or FTEs.

Given that the Act only requires the report to include E-Government initiatives sponsored by OMB, initiatives, this report does not include initiatives funding by "fee-for-service" contributions. "Fee-for-service" contributions represent transfers of funds by partner agencies to initiative service providers in exchange for services rendered by initiative service providers. The amounts are typically based on a transaction/usage-based fee structure (e.g., for payroll processing, payroll service providers base their service fees on the number of employees at a customer agency). Initiative service providers use fees collected from partner agencies to cover ongoing operational costs, perform routine maintenance, and support their customer base.

Agency contributions reflect commitments of funding and/or in-kind services provided by partner agencies to initiative managing partner agencies in support of the initiative or line of business. Contribution amounts are determined annually through collaborative, inter-agency E-Gov initiative governance structures and subject to approval by OMB. In-kind contributions represent the dollar equivalent of contribution of services made by an agency in support of the initiative. Such contributions represent non-cash funding, and may include the contribution of equipment, facilities, software, license fees, FTEs, etc.

This report does not include initiatives funding by "fee-for-service" contributions. "Fee-for-service" contributions represent transfers of funds by partner agencies to initiative service providers in exchange for services rendered by initiative service providers. The amounts are typically based on a transaction/usage-based fee structure (e.g., for payroll processing, payroll service providers base their service fees on the number of employees at a customer agency). Initiative service providers use fees collected from partner agencies to cover ongoing operational costs, perform routine maintenance, and support their customer base.

APPENDIX C
FY 2014 FUNDING BY E-GOVERNMENT INITIATIVE AND LINE OF BUSINESS
(INCLUDES IN-KIND CONTRIBUTIONS)
(Includes In-Kind Contributions)

Initiative	Agency	Contributions (Includes In-Kind)
Budget Formulation and Execution LoB	Department of Agriculture	$95,000
	Department of Commerce	$105,000
	Department of Defense	$105,000
	Department of Education	$105,000
	Department of Energy	$105,000
	Department of Health and Human Services	$105,000
	Department of Homeland Security	$105,000
	Department of Housing and Urban Development	$105,000
	Department of the Interior	$105,000
	Department of Justice	$105,000
	Department of Labor	$105,000
	Department of State	$105,000
	Department of Transportation	$105,000
	Department of the Treasury	$105,000
	Department of Veterans Affairs	$105,000
	U.S. Agency for International Development	$105,000
	U.S. Army Corps of Engineers	$80,000
	Broadcasting Board of Governors	$50,000
	Environmental Protection Agency	$75,000
	Equal Employment Opportunity Commission	$50,000
	General Services Administration	$105,000
	Millennium Challenge Corporation	$50,000
	National Aeronautics and Space Administration	$105,000
	National Science Foundation	$105,000
	Office of National Drug Control Policy	$50,000
	Office of Personnel Management	$105,000
	Securities and Exchange Commission	$50,000
	Small Business Administration	$50,000
Budget Formulation and Execution LoB Total		**$2,545,000**

APPENDIX C
FY 2014 FUNDING BY E-GOVERNMENT INITIATIVE AND LINE OF BUSINESS
(INCLUDES IN-KIND CONTRIBUTIONS)
(Includes In-Kind Contributions)

Initiative	Agency	Contributions (Includes In-Kind)
Disaster Assist Improvement Plan	Department of Agriculture	$136,538
	Department of Commerce	$11,538
	Department of Education	$35,577
	Department of Health and Human Services	$123,379
	Department of Homeland Security	$17,990,000
	Department of Housing and Urban Development	$132,692
	Department of the Interior	$50,962
	Department of Justice	$63,462
	Department of Labor	$104,808
	Department of State	$11,538
	Department of the Treasury	$113,462
	Department of Veterans Affairs	$67,308
	Office of Personnel Management	$41,346
	Small Business Administration	$70,192
	Social Security Administration	$39,423
Disaster Assist Improvement Plan Total		**$18,992,225**
Disaster Management Program	Department of Homeland Security	$11,170,000
Disaster Management Program Total		**$11,170,000**
Federal Asset Sales	General Services Administration	$765,000
Federal Asset Sales Total		**$765,000**
Federal Health Architecture	Department of Defense	$2,656,000
	Department of Health and Human Services	$3,522,000
	Department of Veterans Affairs	$2,094,000
	Social Security Administration	$100,000
Federal Health Architecture Total		**$8,372,000**

APPENDIX C
FY 2014 FUNDING BY E-GOVERNMENT INITIATIVE AND LINE OF BUSINESS
(INCLUDES IN-KIND CONTRIBUTIONS)
(Includes In-Kind Contributions)

Initiative	Agency	Contributions (Includes In-Kind)
Financial Management LoB	Department of Agriculture	$167,510
	Department of Commerce	$95,819
	Department of Defense	$187,342
	Department of Education	$230,616
	Department of Energy	$124,236
	Department of Health and Human Services	$230,616
	Department of Homeland Security	$178,140
	Department of Housing and Urban Development	$230,616
	Department of the Interior	$124,236
	Department of Justice	$124,236
	Department of Labor	$141,399
	Department of State	$95,892
	Department of Transportation	$230,616
	Department of the Treasury	$95,892
	Department of Veterans Affairs	$158,998
	U.S. Agency for International Development	$95,819
	Environmental Protection Agency	$95,819
	General Services Administration	$41,332
	National Aeronautics and Space Administration	$124,236
	Nuclear Regulatory Commission	$41,332
	National Science Foundation	$139,094
	Office of Personnel Management	$41,332
	Small Business Administration	$67,475
	Social Security Administration	$67,475
Financial Management LoB Total		**$3,130,078**

APPENDIX C
FY 2014 FUNDING BY E-GOVERNMENT INITIATIVE AND LINE OF BUSINESS
(INCLUDES IN-KIND CONTRIBUTIONS)
(Includes In-Kind Contributions)

Initiative	Agency	Contributions (Includes In-Kind)
Geospatial LoB	Department of Agriculture	$225,000
	Department of Commerce	$225,000
	Department of Defense	$42,000
	Department of Education	$25,000
	Department of Energy	$50,000
	Department of Health and Human Services	$50,000
	Department of Homeland Security	$225,000
	Department of Housing and Urban Development	$50,000
	Department of the Interior	$800,000
	Department of Justice	$50,000
	Department of State	$50,000
	Department of Transportation	$50,000
	Department of the Treasury	$25,000
	Department of Veterans Affairs	$25,000
	U.S. Agency for International Development	$25,000
	U.S. Army Corps of Engineers	$50,000
	Environmental Protection Agency	$225,000
	General Services Administration	$50,000
	National Aeronautics and Space Administration	$225,000
	National Archives and Records Administration	$15,000
	National Science Foundation	$25,000
	Small Business Administration	$25,000
	Social Security Administration	$25,000
Geospatial LoB Total		**$2,557,000**

APPENDIX C
FY 2014 FUNDING BY E-GOVERNMENT INITIATIVE AND LINE OF BUSINESS
(INCLUDES IN-KIND CONTRIBUTIONS)
(Includes In-Kind Contributions)

Initiative	Agency	Contributions (Includes In-Kind)
Human Resources Management LoB	Department of Agriculture	$260,870
	Department of Commerce	$130,435
	Department of Defense	$260,870
	Department of Education	$65,217
	Department of Energy	$65,217
	Department of Health and Human Services	$130,435
	Department of Homeland Security	$213,526
	Department of Housing and Urban Development	$65,217
	Department of the Interior	$130,435
	Department of Justice	$260,870
	Department of Labor	$65,217
	Department of State	$65,217
	Department of Transportation	$130,435
	Department of the Treasury	$260,870
	Department of Veterans Affairs	$260,870
	U.S. Agency for International Development	$65,217
	Central Intelligence Agency	$65,217
	Environmental Protection Agency	$65,217
	General Services Administration	$65,217
	National Aeronautics and Space Administration	$65,217
	National Science Foundation	$65,217
	Office of Personnel Management	$65,217
Human Resources Management LoB Total		**$2,822,220**
Information Systems Security LoB	Department of Homeland Security	$1,555,590
Information Systems Security LoB Total		**$2,590,000**
Internal Revenue Service Free File	Department of the Treasury	$1,555,590
Internal Revenue Service Free File Total		**$1,555,590**

APPENDIX C
FY 2014 FUNDING BY E-GOVERNMENT INITIATIVE AND LINE OF BUSINESS
(INCLUDES IN-KIND CONTRIBUTIONS)
(Includes In-Kind Contributions)

Initiative	Agency	Contributions (Includes In-Kind)
Recreation One-Stop	Department of Agriculture	$200,000
	Department of the Interior	$200,000
	U.S. Army Corps of Engineers	$200,000
Recreation One-Stop Total		**$600,000**
SAFECOM	Department of Homeland Security	$1,440,000
SAFECOM Total		**$1,440,000**

APPENDIX D: DEVELOPMENT STATUS OF E-GOVERNMENT INITIATIVES AND LINES OF BUSINESS

In accordance with section 732(b)(1) of the Act, this table shows the development status of E-Government initiatives and lines of business as reported by the initiative's managing partner. E-Government initiatives and lines of business are evolutionary in nature. While most initiatives have accomplished their initial goals and achieved operational capability, they have also expanded their goals over time, transitioning from individual projects to more robust programs. These programs are constantly evolving; there is no final date by which initiatives and lines of business are considered to have achieved full operational capability.

The development statuses shown in the table below are reflective of agency budget requests. In cases where FY 2014 funds were requested for planning and design, the development status has been categorized as "Planning." In cases where funds were requested for operations and maintenance, the development status has been categorized as "Operations & Maintenance." In cases where agencies have requested money for both planning and design and operations and maintenance, the development status has been categorized as "Mixed Life Cycle."

APPENDIX D
DEVELOPMENT STATUS OF E-GOVERNMENT INITIATIVES AND LINES OF BUSINESS

Initiative	Development Status
Budget Formulation and Execution LoB	Mixed Life Cycle
Disaster Assist Improvement Plan	Mixed Life Cycle
Disaster Management Program	Operations & Maintenance
Federal Asset Sales	Operations & Maintenance
Federal Health Architecture LoB	Mixed Life Cycle
Financial Management LoB	Planning
Geospatial LoB	Mixed Life Cycle
Human Resources Management LoB	Planning
Information Systems Security LoB	Operations & Maintenance
Internal Revenue Service Free File	Operations & Maintenance
Recreation One-Stop	Operations & Maintenance
SAFECOM	Operations & Maintenance

APPENDIX E: RISKS ASSOCIATED WITH E-GOVERNMENT INITIATIVES AND LINES OF BUSINESS

In accordance with section 732(b)(1) of the Act, this table shows the areas of risk associated with E-Government initiatives and lines of business as reported by the initiative's managing partner. All initiatives are required by *OMB Circular A-11, "Preparation, Submission, and Execution of the Budget"* to have risk management plans. Risk management plans are not available to the public due to their sensitive nature. In addition, all initiatives are required to perform an initial risk assessment, including the risk elements listed below, and demonstrate active management of the risk through the life-cycle of the initiative. The risks shown in this table are associated with the following common areas of risk, found in *OMB Circular A- 11, "Supplement to Part 7 – Capital Programming Guide:"*

- **Technology**
- **Project Schedule and Resources**
- **Business**
- **Organizational and Change Management**
- **Strategic**
- **Security**
- **Privacy**
- **Data**
- **Integration Risks**
- **Project Team Risks**
- **Requirements Risks**
- **Cost Risks**
- **Project Management Risks**

APPENDIX E
RISKS ASSOCIATED WITH E-GOVERNMENT INITIATIVES AND LINES OF BUSINESS

Initiative	Associated Risks
Budget Formulation and Execution LoB	Project Schedule and Resources
	Organizational and Change Management
Disaster Assist Improvement Plan	Technology
	Business
Disaster Management Program	Technology
	Business
	Organizational and Change Management
	Security
	Privacy
	Cost Risks
Federal Asset Sales	Technology
	Project Schedule and Resources
	Organizational and Change Management
	Strategic
	Security
	Privacy
	Data
	Cost Risks
	Project Management Risks
Federal Health Architecture LoB	Technology
	Project Schedule and Resources
	Business
	Organizational and Change Management
	Strategic
	Security
	Privacy
	Data
	Cost Risks
	Project Management Risks
Financial Management LoB	Project Schedule and Resources
	Organizational and Change Management
	Integration Risks
	Project Team Risks

APPENDIX E
RISKS ASSOCIATED WITH E-GOVERNMENT INITIATIVES AND LINES OF BUSINESS

Initiative	Associated Risks
Geospatial LoB	Strategic
	Requirements Risks
	Project Management Risks
Human Resources Management LoB	Technology
	Project Schedule and Resources
	Business
	Organizational and Change Management
	Strategic
	Security
	Privacy
	Data
	Integration Risks
	Cost Risks
	Project Management Risks
Information Systems Security LoB	Project Schedule and Resources
	Business
	Project Management Risks
Internal Revenue Service Free File	N/A - IRS Free File is monitored as part of the IRS Filing Season Readiness
Recreation One-Stop	Technology
	Project Schedule and Resources
	Business
	Organizational and Change Management
	Strategic
	Security
	Privacy
	Data
	Integration Risks
	Cost Risks
	Project Management Risks

APPENDIX E
RISKS ASSOCIATED WITH E-GOVERNMENT INITIATIVES AND LINES OF BUSINESS

Initiative	Associated Risks
SAFECOM	Technology
	Project Schedule and Resources
	Business
	Organizational and Change Management
	Strategic
	Security
	Privacy
	Data
	Integration Risks
	Cost Risks
	Project Management Risks

END NOTES

1 SEC. 732. (a) For fiscal year 2012, no funds shall be available for transfers or reimbursements to the E-Government initiatives sponsored by the Office of Management and Budget prior to 15 days following submission of a report to the Committees on Appropriations of the House of Representatives and the Senate by the Director of the Office of Management and Budget and receipt of approval to transfer funds by the Committees on Appropriations of the House of Representatives and the Senate. (b) The report in subsection (a) and other required justification materials shall include at a minimum—(1) a description of each initiative including but not limited to its objectives, benefits, development status, risks, cost effectiveness (including estimated net costs or savings to the government), and the estimated date of full operational capability; (2) the total development cost of each initiative by fiscal year including costs to date, the estimated costs to complete its development to full operational capability, and estimated annual operations and maintenance costs; and (3) the sources and distribution of funding by fiscal year and by agency and bureau for each initiative including agency contributions to date and estimated future contributions by agency. (c) No funds shall be available for obligation or expenditure for new E-Government initiatives without the explicit approval of the Committees on Appropriations of the House of Representatives and the Senate. _www.gpo.gov/fdsys/pkg/PLAW-112publ74/pdf/PLAW-112publ74.pdf._

2 This report does not provide information regarding the International Trade Process Streamlining initiative, previously managed by the U.S. Department of Commerce, as the initiative and associated websites will be decommissioned at the end of calendar year 2013.

3 Executive Order, Improving Assistance for Disaster Victims, available at _http://www.gpo.gov/fdsys/pkg/WCPD-2006-09-04/pdf/WCPD-2006-09-04-Pg1527.pdf._

www.ingramcontent.com/pod-product-compliance
Lightning Source LLC
Chambersburg PA
CBHW08025290526

45790CB00005B/1817